Yesterday's Tomorrow

Yesterday's Tomorrow

—◆—

Raw Stories *of* Hard-Fought Recovery

BARRY LONGYEAR

Hazelden Publishing

Hazelden Publishing
Center City, Minnesota 55012-0176
800-328-9000
hazelden.org/bookstore

Library of Congress Cataloging-in-Publication Data
L., Barry, 1942–
    Yesterday's tomorrow : recovery meditations for hard cases / Barry L.
        p. cm.
    ISBN 978-1-56838-160-2 Ebook ISBN 978-1-61649-109-3
    1. Twelve-step programs—Meditations. 2. Devotional calendars. I. Title.
BL624.5.L25 1997
616.86'03—dc21   97-15767
                                                                    CIP

24 23 22   6 5 4 3 2

Cover design by Terri Kinne
Typesetting by Percolator
Editorial development: Christian Johnson
Editiorial project manager: Jean Cook

Editor's notes

In the process of being reissued in 2019, *Yesterday's Tomorrow,* formerly sub-
titled *Recovery Meditations for Hard Cases,* has undergone minor editing up-
dates and been retypeset in the Casus Pro font family.

Alcoholics Anonymous and AA are registered trademarks of Alcoholics
Anonymous World Services, Inc. Reference to the Twelve Steps and Twelve
Traditions does not mean that AA has reviewed or approved the contents of
this publication, nor that AA agrees with the views expressed herein.

Material on page 53 comes from *Overeaters Anonymous,* ©1980 by Overeaters Anonymous, Inc. Reprinted by permission of Overeaters Anonymous,
Inc.

This publication is intended to support personal growth and should not
be thought of as a substitute for the advice of health care professionals. The
author's advice and viewpoints are his own.

Author's note

Ah, hell, the book probably doesn't represent my views, either.

Contents

Introduction

So, why the title *Yesterday's Tomorrow: Raw Stories of Hard-Fought Recovery*? Well, for many of us "hard cases," recovery doesn't come all that naturally. We kick, scream, and flail when any nugget of traditional recovery wisdom attempts to enter our brains, making our recoveries a little harder fought than most. But who qualifies as a hard case, and can you count yourself among us? A hard case is a drug addict, alcoholic, compulsive eater, codependent, sex addict, compulsive gambler—or any or all of the above—who has, perhaps, a harder shell when it comes to receiving recovery wisdom. Yesterday's tomorrow is like tomorrow's yesterday: a hard case's convoluted way of saying "today." It all has to do with trying to hit what is for some of us that almost impossible target, the present moment. Hard cases frequently get stuck in the past or in the future, with occasional periods of bouncing back and forth between the two. But there's more than that to being a hard case.

When it comes to prayer, hard cases frequently suffer from paralyzed knees, low-altitude sickness, and a newly discovered interest in those sciences and philosophies which hold forth on rugged individualism. Trust doesn't come easily to a hard case, and trusting in some sort of vaporous power purported to be greater than oneself is an unlikely proposition.

As is trust in just about anything. When I was going through aftercare at a local rehab, I heard one of the patients announce that he wasn't going to go to any Twelve Step meetings after rehab "because they told me to stay away from drunks and junkies." I suspected he might just possibly have been a hard case.

As for meditation, this work could have just as easily been titled *The I Hate to Meditate Book*. The one thing the hard case finds more frightening than trusting a higher power is the hard case trusting in himself or herself. That's what meditation is: listening by yourself, perhaps to yourself or to a higher self, or to a higher power. Where day-to-day recovering persons may slip effortlessly into the lotus position, adopt an expression of celestial bliss, and "Om" their way to enlightenment, the hard case makes jokes. "Meditation is either sleeping and not getting any rest, or resting and not getting any sleep." Or "So it turns out I'm not a sofa spud; I'm spiritual!" Or "Om, Om on the range . . ."

Are we agreed that there are hard cases? Good. So, why this particular book?

I'm a hard case. Through much experimentation, I have learned that I am not unique, that there are a lot of hard cases out there. From my own experience, I know that hard cases need something more than mere slogans, smarmy platitudes, or off-the-cuff suggestions to move them to action. They need to know *what* and *why*, and even more importantly, they need to know *how*. It's all well and good to say "Turn it over" to someone who is flipping flapjacks. A person holding a wildcat by the tail is never in any doubt about how to let go. In recovery, however, when it comes to letting go, hard cases need to be given the letting-go tool itself, complete with written directives and the instructional video. We need to be told and shown how it works; and most important, it needs to be done by someone carrying the scars of experience and done in a manner that can sidestep our rather substantial defenses.

If you come at a hard case with a halo on your head, all you'll do is bore him or her to death. If your wisdom is couched in clichés or in plug-in modules of long-winded psychobabble, the hard case will probably get ill. If the message aimed at a hard case is at all self-righteous or judgmental in content or tone, the almost certain result will be anger or laughter. And if you attempt to shove any part of your religious beliefs down the throat of a hard case, chances are you're going to get a fight. Yet there are many hard cases in recovery. To recover and stay alive, we also need the message, but how is that message going to get through all of our armor?

I always considered myself a man of judgment and reason. I didn't know I was a hard case until after I began my journey of recovery in rehab. Early in the screening process I was somehow sorted out into a last-chance therapy group whose members started out on probation. As a genteel young lady explained it to me, "In this group they're already onto your bullshit and they're tired of it. Screw up once and they toss you out on your ass." In other words, the members of this elite therapy unit were hard cases, or "tough nuts to crack," as one fellow patient put it.

At the time I didn't know why I had been gathered up with the other nuts for this particular honor. Later, while looking at where I had scratched out the Serenity Prayer that had been printed on my coffee cup, I realized that it might have had something to do with my attitude.

My first day in rehab I awakened from my last blackout screaming at a nurse that I didn't have a problem, and even if I did, all of this down-home-Jesus-higher-power crap had not a damned thing to do with me. In addition, I attempted to walk out of treatment on my fourth day, and only remained by the grace of a hellish cold snap and a very large roommate who promised to break my legs if that was what it would take to keep me on the premises. He repeated his offer two days later when I attempted to walk out again. Although my experience shed more than a little light on my friend's control problem, I couldn't really see that I was one of the tough nuts. The recovering psychiatrist who did my initial screening gave me my very first understandable indication. After listening to me go on for an hour about how I didn't have a problem, how I really wasn't like the other people on the unit, and even if I did have a problem, why this Twelve Step gibberish wasn't for me, he shook his head and said, "Barry, you're just bound and determined to make this as hard on yourself as possible, aren't you?"

I was stunned at the suggestion—and disagreed, of course. The reason I disagreed was that I figured such a person as that would have to be stupid, which was not in accordance with my self-image. I later learned that such a person is not stupid; instead, he's a hard case. Hard cases are usually too smart for their own good.

Now, after several decades in recovery, my hard case has a few cracks in it. Still, I have major battles with things that others in the program seem to have no trouble accepting and doing. I wrestle with things like asking for help, trusting a higher power, using the phone, depending on others, trusting the process, letting go, working the Twelve Steps, staying in the present moment, and so on.

I began recovery thinking that my problem was alcohol and prescription drugs. Within two years it finally got through to me that I am also a food addict and a compulsive gambler. By then I also knew I had already earned my stripes in Al-Anon and ACA (Adult Children of Alcoholics or ACOA, now called Adult Children of Alcoholics/Dysfunctional Families or ACA). Over the course of the next few years I had to face up to being an incest survivor, as well. I seemed to be addicted to everything from fingernail biting and video games to butter bread and nasal sprays. Hell, when I stopped smoking I even became addicted to nicotine chewing gum! I ran out of days on which to have meetings some time ago.

Often during the course of this adventure the cracks in my hard case filled in again. It was all too easy for me to think, "Is this what recovery is—every time I struggle to my knees, I get slapped down again? What does the universe have against me?"

I was at the top of my career when I was using but once I got clean, I couldn't get any work. On top of this were serious health problems, tax increases, economic recessions, advancing age, thinning hair, and so on. Black depression haunted me for months on end. It was at exactly such moments when some Goody Two-shoes reading from one of those Polly-anna, everything's-perfect-in-my-life meditation books would leave me grinding my teeth and feeling even more depressed. I must admit, there are times when I feel that the authors of those books are entirely too happy.

"We can't afford resentments, so forgive and forget." These are lame words to someone who is thinking, "If I can get the bastards back before I reach Step Eight, will I still be okay with the program?" In the depths of a pity wallow, though, another member of the fellowship would frequently get through my hard case and help save my sanity by the use of very special, but admittedly unauthorized, program tools: humor, grit, and an occasional spiritual two-by-four upside my head.

For example, shortly after beginning therapy for being an incest survivor, all the rules of the universe seemed to have changed for me. It was like being taken back to my first day in rehab. The shame, the anger, the emptiness, the betrayal, and how all of this affected my loved ones and my view of reality combined to make returning to my old life of puking mindless oblivion look rather attractive. It was at the closing of an NA meeting, my head deep within this chasm of self-pity, when someone began reading that particular group's traditional closing, the third paragraph of "We Do Recover" from *Narcotics Anonymous*. It began, "When at the end of the road we find that we can no longer function as a human being, either with or without drugs, we all face the same dilemma. What is there left to do? There seems to be this alternative: either go on as best we can to the bitter ends—jails, institutions, or death—"

At that point I interrupted by throwing in my cynical two cents by hollering, "Right on!"

In response, a friend at the meeting said, "Remember, Barry, life sucks better clean."

Life sucks better clean. It was funny, it was true, and it was put in terms a hard case like me could understand. I was too far in the hole that night to do anything but sneer at "Today I have a life second to none," or some other attempt at a gratitude wallow. "Life sucks better clean," on the other hand, was right where I was. It was all the reason I needed to stay clean that night. I added that sage remark to the many funny, irreverent, hard-hitting, filthy, and definitely unauthorized program sayings that have saved my life over the years, continuing the growth of what became *Yesterday's Tomorrow*.

The purpose of this book might be easier to understand by stepping outside the program for a moment and taking a clandestine peek into a ski instructor's frustrating session with a student who just doesn't seem to be able to understand anything. Another skier related this tale to me:

"The teenage boy said he wanted to learn to ski fast. He was into speed and just wasn't getting anywhere. His instructor, a tall, heavy-set man, patiently explained why the position in which the boy was holding his skis was slowing him down. Just as patiently he explained how the skis needed to be positioned and used for speed. By the time I came upon these two, I gathered that this was about the fifth time this patient show-and-tell had been performed. The instructor asked the boy if he understood *this time*, the boy nodded, and they gave it another try. Fifty yards down the slope, the instructor screamed *"Stop!"*

"The boy pulled up and the instructor plowed to a stop behind him, showering him with snow. Then the instructor opened his coat, pulled out his shirt-tail, pushed up his goggles, and with wide-open rolling eyes, the big man's arms began swinging around his head, his ski poles dancing wildly in the air, dangerously close to the boy's head. He looked quite insane. Then he bellowed at the boy, much like a mad bull elephant, '*Go*, you blockhead! And if I catch you, I *will kill you!!!*'

"The boy took off down slope, that madman hot on his heels, and did so many things right he probably set a trail speed record."

—◆—

Humor, sarcasm, and irreverence, as well as hard and gritty language, are not everyone's recovery tools. If you require a kinder, gentler, more reverent path through the daily meditation process, there are a great many such guides on the market. Find one, go ye forth, and be serene. However, if you are like me and need a tickle in the ribs, an occasional kick in the butt, and a little grit beneath your wheels to make it up that next hill, *Yesterday's Tomorrow* might be for you.

The astute reader will notice that in this work I do not pretend that Twelve Step programs are efficiently administered organizations staffed by philosopher saints and peopled by angels. These programs were created and made up out of people like me: drunks, junkies, sex fiends, control freaks, and every stripe of degraded, broken bastard that life, evolution, and disease can throw up. We are somewhat less than perfect. That this wrecked mass of humanity established and operates these programs, enabling millions to recover and reclaim their lives as responsible, productive, and whole human beings is only the beginning of the miracle begun in 1935 by Alcoholics Anonymous, the parent of all Twelve Step groups.

As in life, in every Twelve Step program there are problems, imperfections, and four-alarm idiots. Along with recovery, however, come the tools we need to deal with problems, the work we need to eliminate imperfections, and the means we need to accept everybody for who, what, and where they are with serenity. Twelve Step meetings are places of acceptance and love whose products are recovery and reclaimed lives, even for my case-hardened brothers and sisters.

Hard cases need something special, and I hope you find some of what you need in what follows. Very little of this work is original, but only a portion can be credited because most of the authors were and are anonymous. They are part of that vast underground of ambush healers who, to bring a truth into existence, cut through the bull and give the dragon's tail a tweak.

There are, no doubt, things in this modest volume that will offend the political and program correctness police, Mr. & Mrs. Program, and all of the other program officers, blue flamers, and Twelfth Step Adventists. The program has been and remains the lifeline for me and for many of those I love. It is neither my object nor my desire, therefore, either to damage the program or offend anyone. However, each of us sees reality and reports on it through highly individual filters. This is the way I and a number of others in the program see it and work it. For others, this is an excellent opportunity to practice the slogan: "Take what you need and leave the rest." (Come to think of it, I ran into a guy the other night who was offended by *that* slogan. He called it "working the program cafeteria-style." Well, as the recovery program recruiting poster says, "Brain Damage: It's not just a disease; it's an adventure!")

I have used no names of persons in Twelve Step programs who are quoted, not even first names. This has been for purposes of anonymity and to avoid confusion and misunderstanding. Through the years exactly who said what first has gotten rather dim.

Someone drops a zinger into a sharing session and some of those who hear it repeat it at other meetings and sharing sessions where still others pick it up and spread it to even more meetings across the face of the globe. Although each one of these gems must have had at some time and place an original author, there is no way to track down the responsible parties. To these anonymous angels of the dark side, therefore, this book is gratefully dedicated.

1. The Road to Hell

A person new in the program, proud to show how he was making his life better, showed his sponsor the list of New Year's resolutions he had spent the previous day writing. His sponsor adjusted his glasses and read:

This year I resolve
- *to lose twenty-five pounds*
- *to exercise thirty minutes twice each day*
- *to finish the remodeling on my house*
- *to get a new car*
- *to increase my income by at least 20 percent*
- *to read at least six books every month*
- *to go to a meeting every day*
- *to do steps one through nine*
- *to call my sponsor every day*
- *to pray and meditate every morning and night*
- *to form only healthy relationships*
- *never to drink, drug, or eat compulsively ever again*

His sponsor handed back the note and said, "Hell, son. That's not a list of New Year's resolutions. It's a goddamned suicide note."

There is an excellent reason why not one of the Twelve Step programs uses as a slogan "One *year* at a time" or "One *lifetime* at a time." More than half a century of experience shows that it doesn't work. What works is "One *day* at a time," and some of us even have to shave this down to one hour or minute at a time.

If we attempt to take on our life's problems all at once, sooner or later we will go down in flames. The disease is hellishly patient. The dragon is always waiting for us to put unrealistic expectations on ourselves, gleefully helping us to become miserable failures so we can go out and return to the nightmare.

Never is a long, long time. Just for today, however, I can work my program, doing the best I can to take care of myself and meet my obligations, knowing as I do that humility is the Heimlich maneuver for biting off more than I can chew.

2. Confusion Is Okay

"I don't understand it," admitted a woman at a meeting. "I used to be very sharp, making important decisions every day. Now that I've gotten into the program, it's a good day when I can put my pantyhose on with the toes pointing the right way. I'm so confused."

Her sponsor said, "Confusion is okay. Back when you had all the answers you were in big trouble."

— ◆ —

When the disease is active, the dragon has a field day because it makes us so certain about everything:

"I work hard! I deserve to relax with a [drink, drug, smoke, box of chocolates, poker game, etc.]."

"You're the one with the problem! Not me!"

"If I don't take care of him [her or it] who will?"

"I can handle it."

"I can quit whenever I want."

"I can't get a break."

"If I don't control him [her, it] no one will be in control."

"I can do it by myself."

"Things will never get any better."

"Things can't possibly get any worse."

"The only answer is for you [or me] to leave."

"I *need* a [drink, drug, smoke, box of chocolates, poker game, etc.]."

And so on.

A reality check happens every time the things we're so certain about blow up in our faces because the real world won't go along with our fantasies. I wasn't at all confused my first day in rehab. I knew I didn't have a problem. Three days later, crippled by withdrawal pains and terrorized by hallucinations, I learned that I just might be in error. It seems I *did* have a problem. That's when things began being very confused, because all of the old rules no longer worked and a new set needed to be learned.

Today I don't have to know it all, I don't have to have all the answers, and I don't have to be certain about a damned thing. All I need to remember is that I have a disease that will make me miserable and kill me if I don't take my medicine: meetings, not using, working the Steps, and asking for help. Everything else will become clearer in time.

Or not. As one person said at a meeting: "It's been seven years in recovery and I still don't know what's going on. I'm having a whole lot better time at it, though."

3. On Pouring Water from a Bucket

It has been said many times that everyone in AA also ought to be in Al-Anon. Similar things have been said regarding other Twelve Step groups. The addict should also be in Nar-Anon, the recovering gambler also ought to be in Gam-Anon, and so on. Many of us come from families affected by this disease: parents, spouses, siblings, and children. There is another important relationship that needs help, as well—our relationship with ourselves. Since we live with ourselves and must rebuild this relationship to recover, there is a lot we need to know about how to live with a genuine sicko. Still, the most frequent cry in any recovery program, however, is "How can I get my wife [husband, parents, children] into Al-Anon [Nar-Anon, Gam-Anon, etc.]?"

It is a family disease. It doesn't matter who uses the substances or makes the bets—everyone is affected. Addicts and alkies don't understand this until they get into recovery. As we become healthier mentally, it becomes pretty damned obvious that everyone who was close to us is sick. At one meeting in the dead of a Maine winter, the sharing went like this:

"I can see what my wife is doing to herself. My god, she is obsessed with controlling everything. It doesn't matter what I do—she's there criticizing, instructing, and usually taking over with a guilt-flinging 'Never mind, I'll do it!' There is nothing I can do that is right, as far as she's concerned. It's not only driving me crazy, it's already driven her crazy!"

Another man nodded and said, "I know what you mean. Yesterday I finally blew up at her. She told me to fill the humidifier and I filled a bucket and went to the humidifier. I didn't even have the top off before she was telling me to be careful. I lifted the bucket and began pouring and she began telling me where to pour the water, how to hold the pail, and how to tilt the thing. Finally I just screamed at her, 'I can pour water out of a goddamned bucket!' She could really use Al-Anon. *I* could really use her being in Al-Anon!" He thought for a moment, his eyebrows went up, and he blurted out, "Hell, *I* could really use Al-Anon!"

4. The First Word

I was absolutely miserable. I hadn't used alcohol or other drugs for two years, I was closing on my first year of being abstinent from compulsive overeating, I hadn't been in a game or made a bet for over a year, and I was edging into my second month without nicotine or caffeine. Despite all of this immaculate living, I was having dark thoughts. I was in a panic and didn't know what to do. I was driven to make one of my very rare telephone calls to my sponsor, and we got together the next day.

He listened to my tale of woe and said, "You're absolutely right. It is tough to see that next step when you have your head up your ass."

Before my anger could move my jaw into gear, he continued. "Look at what you've been telling me. *I* don't drink. *I* don't drug. *I* don't overeat. *I* don't gamble. *I* don't smoke. *I* don't use caffeine. No wonder you're miserable. You're a one-dude program." He pulled out a wrinkled card printed with the Twelve Steps and dropped it in front of me. "You see that first word in the Twelve Steps?"

A little confused, I looked at the card and said, "Yeah. The first word is 'We.'"

"Do you see anywhere in the Steps where it says 'I'?" I shook my head. He tapped the card with his finger. "The most important word in the Twelve Steps is 'we.' This isn't a *me* program; it's a *we* program. *I* can't do it by myself. *We* can. You don't have to fight the gorilla by yourself, which is just as well, because you can't. Hitch yourself up to that 'we,' otherwise that 'I' is going to kill you. That's the program's Step Zero."

After that I made it a "we" program instead of a "me" program, the panic was over, and the program began working for me.

— ◆ —

There is a lot more to recovery than being abstinent from a substance or behavior. There is learning a new way of life that involves helping and being helped by others. Today I don't have to fight the dragon by myself. In fact, with the help of my brothers and sisters in the program, I no longer have to fight at all. Every program's version of the Twelve Steps begins with "We." It's for a reason.

5. Beginner's Kit

"Don't use, go to meetings, and ask for help," said a person at a meeting. In a nutshell, it's the beginner's recovery kit. It is a simple remedy for complicated people. Whatever your substance or behavior is, don't act out, go to your program meetings, and ask for help. Get help from the meeting, from a sponsor, from a power that is stronger than your disease. It's so simple, but sometimes it's too simple to understand.

For example, another person at the meeting answered that statement by saying, "I have a brain trained to rationalize using again and again when I know good and well that using will destroy me and consume everyone and everything I value. Simple rationalizations haven't worked for years. I need complexity, a labyrinth of cause and effect so mind-numbing that the truth can get lost in it forever. That's why when I hear 'Don't use,' the next words out of my mouth are, 'Yeah, but . . . .'"

"Don't use," repeated the first person.

"Yeah, but what if my car breaks down? What if I get in a fight with my boss? What if I get bad news from my doctor? What if I lose my job? What if I can't pay my bills? What if the people I owe money to send leg-breakers after me? What if my life partner leaves me? What if my life partner stays and abuses me? What if my dog gets run over? What if an earthquake swallows my house? What if the world's leaders freak and trigger off a nuclear holocaust? What if everything and everybody in the world gangs up against me? What then?"

"Don't use," the first person repeated a second time. "Even if your ass falls off, don't use. There is *no* reason good enough."

The second person clasped his hands together, looked at the floor, and said, "Yeah, but what if I can't stop?"

The first person raised his eyebrows, shrugged, and held out his hands as he said, "Oh, well in that case you need a miracle. But don't worry about that. Twelve Step programs depend upon miracles. To get one working for you, don't use, go to meetings, and ask for help."

— ◆ —

Just for today I'll try to be simple enough to recover.

6. Moments of Silence

At the beginning of every meeting, the chairperson usually opens the session by calling for a moment of silence followed by the Serenity Prayer. Depending on the person holding the chair, this moment can last as little as a few seconds or as long as a minute or two. When I first came into the program I had absolutely no idea what to do during such moments except be uncomfortable. The fact that I was uncomfortable during communal silences prompted my therapist to suggest that I spend the time trying to get in touch with what it was that was making me uncomfortable. That was when I learned how much of my time I had spent filling my life with noise.

I usually had music or the television on, or I was filling the air with my own words. All of this, of course, was meant to drown out what I was feeling inside. In other words, I used noise like a drug. Ever since learning that, I use those moments of silence to listen to myself.

A friend uses the time to say a small prayer. He says to himself, "Help me to hear your message. Help me to carry your message." If the moment of silence is so short he can only say the first part, he figures it's a sign for him to spend the meeting with his mouth shut and his ears open.

Another person in the program uses the time to ask himself why he is there. If his answers come up lame, he shares about it at the meeting. Some use the time to be grateful for recovery and that night's meeting. Some say, "Help me to help." Still others clean their fingernails, wiggle their feet, take a snooze, or stare impatiently at the nearest time-piece. There's nothing right or wrong about any of these ways of spending moments of silence. It is an individual program.

Then there are assigned moments of silence where the chairperson asks those at the meeting to remember why they are there or to keep a sick program brother or sister in mind. The importance of such moments became clear one night after a meeting of painful and honest sharing. The meeting closed with a group hug, then the chairperson said, "Let's have a moment of silence for the still-suffering addict."

"Who just might be standing next to you," added a small voice.

It's as good a way as any to ask for help.

7. The Proper Equipment

There are piles of suggestions in the program. We get them in program literature, we get them at meet-ings, and we get them from sponsors, friends, and from higher powers. However, they are only sugges-tions. This is mainly because all one has to do to get an addict to refuse to do something is to tell him that he *must* do it.

The program suggests "Don't use, go to meetings, and ask for help." It also suggests staying away from old using friends and places. It suggests putting off any big relationship changes for the first year. And it suggests praying, meditating, using a sponsor, using the phone, getting involved in service work, and working the Twelve Steps. True, they are only suggestions. However, as one program brother put it, "The program suggestions are like the word 'Pull' on a parachute's D-ring. It's only a suggestion, but if you don't take it, you better come up with another answer *fast.* "

8. The Great Mind-Opener

Many of us came into the program with our minds shut like steel vaults. When I first learned about going to meetings, getting a sponsor, and relying on others in the program, I said to myself, "That's out of the question." I was uncomfortable around others, and I couldn't even imagine trusting anyone other than myself. My mind stayed closed until the pain of trying recovery on my own forced me to reconsider my decision. As Marcel Proust wrote, "To kindness, to knowledge, we make promise only; pain we obey."

Pain is the great mind-opener. I wasn't willing even to consider that I might have a problem until the painful consequences of my disease moved me to review the issue. Every major period of growth in the program for me has been preceded by an amount of pain sufficient to make changing my way of doing things the more attractive path. If I can achieve and maintain an open mind, if I can always be teachable, I can avoid a lot of pain by learning from the experiences of others. Today I work on opening my mind by experiencing fully the painful consequences of having a closed one.

9. A Special Secret

Just as there are no successful ways to force someone into recovery, there are no successful ways to force anyone into Al-Anon, Nar-Anon, or any other support group. Support groups such as these are not programs for people who need them; they're programs for those who want them. There are ways to carry the message, however. I learned one method at an Al-Anon meeting. The speaker was sharing how her husband had gotten into Twelve Step recovery, and how trying to control his life and discover his special secret led her to her own recovery.

"I would constantly search through the house, the garage, and the garden looking at all of his old hiding places, looking for that bottle I knew he had. I'd question him about where he was going, demand an accounting of where he'd been, check up on what he was up to, and sit up nights to make sure he didn't leave the house after I went to sleep. One night he came home, from a meeting—he *said*—and went straight up to the bedroom. After that, he came downstairs to make himself some coffee. He had obviously hidden something in the bedroom. Why else sneak into the house like that?

"I was determined to find out what his secret was. While he was busy with the coffeepot, I went upstairs and began searching. I searched the closet, beneath the bed, between the mattress and the box springs, the night stands, and the wastebasket. Then I looked in the bureau. What he had hidden was in the bureau beneath his clean underwear and socks: a white envelope filled with something. That night, after he was asleep, I took the envelope downstairs, went to the kitchen, and steamed it open. It was filled with Al-Anon literature and a meeting list."

10. Bring Your Ass

For a long time when I was new in the program, I had only one tool. I went to the meetings. I didn't have a sponsor, I didn't use the telephone, I didn't read the literature, I didn't work the Steps, and my idea of a higher power was a vague reference to "the program," which I never used as a source of help. I was afraid of many things. I was afraid of the others in the program, I was afraid that I really wasn't worth anyone else's time or concern, and I was absolutely terrified of being rejected.

It is possible to stay clean by doing nothing but going to meetings. However, it is a rough road. I kept to that road, however, and learned from others at the meetings that there is a better way. As one person put it, "If all your problems were nails, the only tool you'd need would be a hammer." Little by little at the meetings I learned about the other program tools. As I overcame my fears and began to trust just a little, I began to share. I read the literature, I did a little service work, went on Twelfth Step calls, got a sponsor, called people between meetings, and worked the Twelve Steps of recovery. Once I got on my knees and asked a power greater than myself to help me, I was the only one who was surprised when, all of a sudden, I was sharing in this wondrous thing called *serenity*. As one person pointed out in reference to meetings, "All you have to do is bring your ass. Your mind and heart will eventually follow."

11. The Banana That Got Away

"I need to watch where I'm walking," shared an old-timer. "The further I back away from the edge of that cliff, the closer I might be getting to the edge of another cliff."

He shared that night about how he worked the program so well that he eventually discovered he could skip a meeting or two and would still be clean and serene. "There are lots of tools other than meetings, so who needed them? Skipping a few meetings freed up my evenings and gave me a lot more time with my family to do things I wanted to do. After a few months of this, I stopped going to meetings altogether. A few weeks after that I looked at myself, still clean and serene, and decided that I had been proven right. I no longer needed meetings. A little over a year later I had lost my family, job, home, and car and was screaming out my guts in a detox center."

Another addict at the meeting clasped his hands over his belly and nodded as he said, "Yep. Them's what don't go to meetings don't get to hear what happens to them's what don't go to meetings. That's why they say to keep coming back. It's only the banana that gets away from the bunch that gets skinned."

12. Do I Really Need a Meeting?

A person was sharing that she really didn't believe in "slips." She said, "A slip sounds like 'Oops, I didn't see that oily spot on the sidewalk.' A relapse is different. Every relapse I've had or seen was planned out months in advance. It's like sneaking out the night before, pouring motor oil all over the front steps, then 'slipping' when you go to work the next morning. They're more like jumps than slips, and they always seem to begin with cutting out meetings. The dragon is sneaky, so we're not always aware of the planning, but it's there. That's why I need meetings, to blow away the dragon smoke."

Sooner or later everyone is tempted to cut back on meetings or to skip them altogether. This doesn't mean you always wind up in a detox ward, but it does always deny the others at the meetings of the absent addict's presence. The help was there and freely given when I needed it, and being at the meeting is one form of service I can do to share this wonderful gift of my recovery with others. Today I can remember that I may not always need a meeting, but the meetings always need me.

13. Putting Down the Paddle

The regulars at the meeting had heard this line from this same person a dozen times or more, each time just before he was preparing to go out and use again. "I needed every last drink, drug, and destructive act that brought me here," he said. "I've had a lot of slips, but this time I'm back for good. This time I've really hit my bottom."

"You know," drawled a voice from the back of the room, "if you hit your bottom often enough they call it a spanking."

14. How to Bury a Bone

Two friends in the program were talking, and the first person had just finished describing how his boss had verbally assaulted him two days before. "I don't know what it is," he continued. "I keep telling myself that it has nothing to do with me, how it really is unimportant, and 'let go and let God.' Still, it's gnawing at the back of my head. I keep turning it over but it keeps coming back."

His friend said, "You sound like a dog trying to bury a bone without biting it. You've got to pick it up before you can let it go."

Marcel Proust wrote, "We are healed of a suffering only by experiencing it to the full." I knew a person who used to put it differently. In rehab my counselor used to greet patients and family members by saying, "I wish you a lot of pain." This statement more than once drew a raised eyebrow and a response of, "Uh, thanks a heap," as the respondee anxiously looked about for the white coats who would take that very strange counselor away to Happy Valley. Even so, as time has passed in the program I've learned what they meant. There is no healing without feeling.

As one addict put it, "It's like a rotten tooth. If you get it pulled it's going to hurt like hell for a short time, but then the pain is gone. If you don't get it pulled, it's going to hurt and make you sick forever."

No one gets into the program without injury. For today I welcome the pain that is necessary for me to recover.

Mostly.

15. Where I'm Supposed to Be

It was at a small meeting on a gloomy evening in the depths of a Maine winter. Most of those sharing were all on the same subject. "I've got such-and-such years in the program but I'm not where I ought to be."

"So this is recovery, huh? Day after day with no excitement of any kind. Where's the payoff?"

"When I first came into the program it seemed so exciting, but now it's all old stuff."

"Where is all of this serenity that's supposed to land on me?"

And so on. No one appeared to be happy where he or she was, including the new person who shared. He had been silent during the meeting, but after he introduced himself and told us why he was there, the effect on the meeting was electric.

"I'm a heroin addict," he began. "Eight years ago I stopped using heroin because I was afraid of losing my job. To help me through it, I drank, and I've been drinking ever since. My problem right now is that the drinking is getting way out of control and I'm afraid of losing my job again. What I need from you people is this: how do I control the drinking until I can retire and go back to heroin?"

We didn't have any answers that he was willing to hear, but he gave all of us a valuable gift. After listening to him there wasn't a single addict in the room who wasn't exceedingly grateful for where he or she was in the program.

—◆—

For today I am grateful for everyone who shares at meetings. Without their examples of what does and does not work, I am on my own. On my own I don't work at all.

16. Admit or Accept?

Step One says, "We admitted we were powerless over our addiction [substance, compulsion], that our lives had become unmanageable."

After a four-month return to the addictive wilds, one of the lucky ones who managed to make it back to the program alive said, "I don't get it. I took the First Step. I admitted I was powerless and that my life was unmanageable."

"You admitted it," said his sponsor, "But maybe you didn't quite get around to *accepting* it."

To someone new in the program, especially after coming off a four-month binge, distinctions between "accept" and "admit" sometime seem a bit confusing. Many of us don't want to look stupid, however, and so we answer, "Right. That was my problem all along." Later, when we're by ourselves, we frown, scratch our heads, and mutter, "What in hell was he talking about?"

"Admit" and "accept" are different ends of the same pipe. One definition of "admit" says that it means "to accept as true." Similarly, one definition of "accept" says that it means "to regard as true." What we need to know to recover, however, sometimes comes from strange places. Curiously enough, the Latin root for "admit" means "to send" and the Latin root for "accept" means "to receive." In other words, for some of us, admitting our powerlessness means that we've told this to others. Accepting it, however, means that we've let ourselves in on this vital piece of information.

—◆—

It made me think of my own battle with reality in rehab. Three days of yelling at everyone, "I don't have a problem," followed by that bone-crushing withdrawal and the admission that I did have a problem. I remember saying to my roommate that night, "I have never before felt so defeated."

He nodded and answered, "That's why they say to watch out for that First Step. It's a big one."

—◆—

Today admitting my powerlessness over my addictions is as easy as saying "Good morning" to someone. Accepting it, however, is and will always be my first and most important task of the day. As that great sage Popeye once said, "I yam what I yam." Just as soon as I forget that, I'm on my way back to the nightmare.

17. Power Play

A man in a big hurt once made his way into a meeting and shared his story with us. After he was finished, he said he definitely had a problem with pot. The weed was choking every aspect of his life out of existence and he was powerless to stop it. This looked like a pretty good First Step to me until one of the old-timers said, "I heard your story, and I was just wondering if you think you might have a problem with alcohol too."

The guy emphatically shook his head. "No. The booze is under control. When I've had enough to drink, I pass out."

Some of us began laughing until it became clear that he wasn't kidding.

I witnessed another version of the same thing. This inquiring mind wanted to know how to get off cocaine. His use of pot, however, was no problem. "After all," he added, "pot is only psychologically addictive."

Someone at the meeting then asked, "So when are you getting your brain transplant?"

18. Putting God in the Driver's Seat, and Other Highway Nightmares

Shared one person at a meeting: "I am powerless over all people, places, and things."

"You must be scary as hell on the highway," remarked an old-timer. When asked to explain what he had meant by his comment, the old-timer said, "I have lots of power. This morning I got up by myself, washed, dressed, and fed myself, drove myself to work, made three really big sales, did grocery shopping, ate dinner, and made it here for the meeting. That's power. I also have the power to empty booze out of bottle A, pour it into glass B, and dump the stuff down drain C.

"What I don't have power over," he continued, "is my disease. I didn't ask for it, I couldn't stop it, and I can't get rid of it. But if I take that first drug, at *that* moment I become powerless over everything."

—◆—

Another person once said at a meeting, "Humility is simply understanding and accepting the facts of reality. An addict saying he has control over drugs is living out a suicidal fantasy. A recovering addict who says he is powerless over everything has given up life as a human being."

Every now and then I run into another version of super-powerlessness. "I cannot change myself. Only my higher power can change me." This, curiously enough, is often a rationalization for not changing at all. In well-intentioned attempts at becoming or appearing "higher power-centered," some addicts claim this dogmatic powerlessness over changing themselves, often followed by the more astonishing claim that counselors, therapists, psychiatrists, and rehabs are useless. After one such statement, an old-timer responded by saying, "Speaking for myself, there are many things about myself that I can change. I can change how I look at things, I can change my attitude, and I can change my goals. Thanks to modern surgery I can even change how I look. One thing I am powerless over, though, is written down in the First Step."

—◆—

Thus the parable of the man and the flood. The devout fellow is standing on his rooftop, the water rising around him, and he prays for his higher power to save him. As the waters lap at his feet, a rescuer in a rowboat comes by and calls for the man to get in.

"No," the man answers, "my higher power will save me."

The water rises to his waist and two rescuers in a power boat come by and call out to the man to get in. "No," he answers, "my higher power will save me."

The water rises until all but his head is submerged. A rescue helicopter hovers over the man and one of the crew lets down a ladder and calls to the man to grab onto it. "No," the man answers, "my higher power will save me."

The water closes over the man's head and he drowns. When he gets to Heaven he says to his higher power, "Why am I dead? I prayed and prayed and prayed for you to save me."

And his higher power answered: "I sent you two boats and a chopper, you jerk. Why in the hell didn't you use them?"

— ◆ —

As our old friend Anon Y. Mous once said, "If you are powerless over everything, then you aren't responsible for anything." Today I see the danger in taking on the false humility of absolute powerlessness. If I do not have the power to choose and to use the many tools and avenues of recovery around me, I'm dead.

19. The Act and How It Plays

The second part of Step One wanted me to admit that my life was unmanageable. What made this particularly hard for me was the disease's ability to provide me with a very selective memory. I could remember that the year I went into rehab I made more money than any year before or since, while conveniently disregarding getting drunk and falling off my riding lawn mower. The mower and I rolled down a steep slope, the machine drove itself over my legs, and left some of the most interesting scrollwork on my shins. I could remember having a house. What faded in memory, however, is how much of the time I spent breaking windows, shredding paintings, punching holes in walls and doors, and later repairing what I could and mourning the rest.

In rehab, writing my first Step required me to give examples of how better living through chemistry had affected my physical and mental health, my emotional life, my social life, my family relationships—including my sex life—my spirituality, and my occupation. It seemed that Step One didn't really apply to me. My health was just fine, my emotions were dead, I had no social, family, or sex life, spirituality didn't apply to me, and I was still making money. It was later that I remembered how alcohol, fat, stress, overwork, and tobacco helped me into a heart attack at the age of thirty-six and how the heart attack introduced me to the wonderful world of prescription drugs. I remembered working up multiple prescriptions, drunk driving, and how I was putting the lives of others in danger.

When I came into rehab I had three states of being: rage, despair, and unconsciousness. Love was something I could neither give nor accept. Almost everything within me was dead, and the parts that weren't dead were planning on committing murder.

I remembered hating my next-door neighbor for no reason and being afraid to step outside because of the motorists driving by. There was the night after coming home from an awards ceremony where I had the adulation of my fellow writers and had received the applause and approval of thousands of fans. And there I was, sitting with a gun in my mouth, getting ready to put an end to it because all of that approval and recognition wasn't enough. Shortly after that I entered rehab and the program and found out that, yes indeed, my life was unmanageable.

Today I keep Step One in the front of my awareness. If I ever forget what my using life was like and what brought me there, I'll forget as well that there are very good reasons for not picking up and going back to the nightmare.

20. Perrier . . . and Leave the Bottle

A new person in the program was sharing about a birthday party for his father he had attended the day before. "I've only been in recovery for three months, and I was nervous about going to the party. I knew there would be drinking, and it did bother me. I was off in a corner drinking a glass of soda when this guy with a can of beer in his hand comes up to me and says, 'Want a beer?'

"I said, 'No. I can't drink that stuff. I'm an alcoholic.'

"The guy looked puzzled for a moment, then his face lit up and he said, 'Well, I got some whiskey out in the truck.'"

Today it's good for me to remember that no one who hasn't walked the same path as mine understands my recovery. At parties what I need to remember is don't use, bring a friend in the program if possible, and bring my own transportation. I don't ever want my life to depend on someone else's lack of understanding of my needs.

21. The Responsibility for Recovery

Back when we were using, no one—including ourselves—understood our disease. For some reason, though, once we get into recovery we become surprised, shocked, or offended when others don't understand what we're trying to do.

One time when I had a serious sinus infection I went to a doctor. This was the first time I'd ever seen this doctor, and I was given one of those disease-a-thon forms to fill out. Under allergies I wrote, "Drug addict—no mood-altering drugs, including anything containing alcohol."

After examining me the doctor said, "I'm putting you on an antibiotic and how about some codeine for the pain?"

Just in case he had overlooked my note on his form, I replied, "I'm a recovering addict. I can't risk taking something like codeine."

"Oh, this is all right," he said. "It's not in liquid form. These are capsules." What a comfort.

"I'm an addict," I protested.

He frowned and said, "You know, it's not addictive if you take it according to the prescription."

Then I lost it. I smacked myself in the head and said, "No shit? You mean I've been doing it wrong all these years?"

A friend in the program had a similar incident. When the doctor became completely exasperated, he shouted, "When are you people going to learn that you don't have to abuse every drug that comes along?"

My friend shouted back at him, "When are *you* people going to learn that if I take one of those damned pills, I don't have any choice?"

Parents, wives, husbands, children, friends, associates, and anyone else not in recovery cannot fully understand this aspect of our lives. At times they may become impatient with what we have to do to grow in recovery, and may even become abusive by ridiculing the program, putting down meetings, and even trying to tempt us back into using again. If we hinge our recovery on everyone understanding our disease and approving of what we have to do to recover, very few of us will survive. Today I understand that only I am responsible for my own recovery.

22. The View from the Rim

"Why did it happen to me?" wailed a newcomer. Since all of us at one time or another had sung the same song, we listened. Part of the growth that makes recovery possible is saying "Ouch" when we're injured, and nothing damaged us quite as much as our disease. Still, when months later the person is still singing the same song, someone might gently suggest that he might profit by letting go of the self-pity. Of course no one likes to get caught in a pity festival, and we have a tendency to get defensive when found out. Over the years, therefore, several gentle ways of suggesting a self-pity problem have been devised.

> "When the stink gets bad enough, you'll move
> off the pity pot."
> "Dial 1-800-WAAAAAH."
> "Keep listening to that self-pity station,
> WHYY."
> "It's time to throw in the crying towel."
> "When you find yourself in the bottom of a
> hole, stop digging."
> "Recovery's a dirty job, but somebody's got
> to do it."
> "Get off the cross; we need the wood."

"Why me?" is a question without an answer. The unauthorized program corruption of Taoism, "Shit happens," is all the answer there is. In reality's stew of circumstances and events, some good things and some rotten things land on everyone, or as Longfellow put it, "Into each life some rain must fall." Good and bad; don't take either personally. As the turkeys say, "Thanksgiving happens."

—◆—

There are many things we can do when we find ourselves looking at the world from the rim of the pity pot. Share at a meeting, talk to a sponsor, and *listen* to the responses. We can write about it, meditate on it, pray about it, and take positive action to move out of the stink. We can help ourselves by helping another. We can focus on the things we have to be grateful for. We can remember that the dragon has only one job, and that is to make us miserable enough to go back and use. Self-pity is one of the critter's most effective tools to help us kill ourselves. For today I can remember to say "ouch" when I'm hurt, keeping in mind the dangers of becoming a career oucheologist.

23. Changing the Sail

The rehab I went to featured a regular program of return visits. I was back for my six-month return visit, and after our patient group was over for the day, three of us decided to go downtown to see the sights. We were waiting in the middle of a complex of hospitals at the bus stop when a young blind woman walked up, said "Hello," and waded right in telling us about how excited she was to be learning Braille. That's when we learned that she had been blinded only six months earlier. Then she asked why we were there in hospital central.

We looked at each other, wrestled silently with shame and anonymity issues, then we told her we were back for return visits at the drug rehab center. She congratulated us all and gave each of us a big hug. Meanwhile, I was thinking, "Lady, who do you think you're kidding to be handing out all of these big support gestures?" She was *blind*. It was the easiest thing in the world for me to imagine myself blind and lost in hopeless self-pity.

When we got on the bus, it turns out that the driver knew her and that she knew most of the passengers and where they were sitting. She introduced them to us, and at each stop she introduced the new passengers, as well. She inquired how each patient's treatment was progressing, she told jokes, and advised us on some of the places downtown that we really shouldn't miss. I looked at the faces of those on the bus and many of them had the same puzzled expression I must have had on my face. I watched that woman for so long that it finally got through to me. She wasn't kidding anyone. She simply didn't have a second to waste on self-pity. She was living the Serenity Prayer, accepting the things she couldn't change and changing the things she could. She had been dealt a really lousy bunch of cards, but she was playing them to the best of her ability—and winning.

Today when I'm tempted to slide into a wallow of self-pity, I remember that woman at the bus stop and what I heard from someone else at a meeting a few years later. "If you don't like the way you're sailing, don't curse the wind; change your sail."

24. There Is Death in a Name

In AA it's called *red chip fever*. In NA it's called *orange tag freakout*. Every Twelve Step program has its own variation of the thirty-day wonder who, with jaw set, eyes bright, and heart all a-thump, gets the call and decides to spread the word of recovery to suffering humanity. "I have discovered this wonderful gift," cries the tag-struck. "I'll tell the world!"

From experience, as reflected in Tradition Eleven, Twelve Step programs have learned that leaping into a public forum and holding forth upon personal recovery (and how I did it) injures the program by keeping newcomers away. There are several cases of famous athletes, movie stars, and other celebrities who have broken their anonymity in well-intentioned efforts to carry the message. A number of these folks, however, have later gone back out or have paraded sick and bizarre behaviors in front of the cameras, conveying to potential newcomers the wrong message. The price for the addict who, for this reason, refuses to make it into that first meeting, is, of course, a life of hell on the way to an inevitable and quite painful death. As a sponsor once said to me, "Enthusiasm among those young in recovery is endearing, wonderful, and remarkably catching. Enjoy it, be grateful for it, share it with your fellow recoverers, and in your own name, especially before a public forum, shut up about it."

25. Fame and Recovery

Gossip is an addiction. Sometimes at meetings things happen, certain things are shared, or certain persons attend; and you almost bust a gut not sharing it with someone else. At a meeting once someone I hadn't met before recognized me and asked me if I was so-and-so the writer. I said I was, and he said that in his home group there was another writer who was in the program. "Very famous," he added.

I said that there were lots of famous people in the program.

"No," he protested as his eyebrows arched, "I mean this guy is *famous*." A tic was beginning to develop in his left eye.

"That's what I said."

"No, you don't understand." The tic in his eye was getting quite pronounced. Perspiration was beading on his forehead. "Famous. I mean *really* famous! Really *really* famous!"

I knew the writer he was talking about, but it was hypnotic watching this guy. It was like seeing someone who couldn't make up his mind which way to jump sliding down the edge of a giant razor blade. So I asked, "Really really *really* famous?"

"Yes!" he shouted, his face as red as a tomato. "My god, he ... it's ... you know, it's ..."

Finally I took pity on him. "I know who you're talking about," I said.

"Thank God!" he shouted, collapsing from the resolution of his impossible dilemma.

— ◆ —

There are many amusing, hilarious, and even scary stories involving anonymity, but the truth of the matter is that breaking the anonymity of other members costs lives. It wasn't until *after* I got through the meeting doors that I learned that addiction is a disease and nothing to be ashamed of. Before then, the thought that friends, family members, co-workers, or employers might learn that I was going to meetings and, therefore, that I might have a problem was enough to keep me away and keep me dying. We've all heard it before, but it is one of the most important things said at any Twelve Step meeting: "Who you see here, what you hear here, let it stay here." To which most of us usually answer, "Hear! Hear!"

26. Being Human Is Not a Character Defect

I had several years in the program when some severe problems that landed on me all at once had my head running with the squirrels. That night at the meeting, I shared about my problems, how they had affected me, and what I was doing about them. After the meeting, feeling much better, I was on my way to the coffeepot when one of the newer members asked to talk to me. She looked very rattled, her eyes wide and frightened. She said, "Your sharing tonight upset me terribly. You know, those of us at this meeting depend upon you to be here and to be strong for us."

I could feel my eyebrows climbing to my hairline. "Then you're in goddamn big trouble, aren't you?"

She was offering me a whole bunch of power that wasn't mine. Besides, I may not always be there, and I didn't get into this club by being strong.

— ◆ —

There was a time, during my first year in the program, when I believed that to be in recovery meant loving everyone, being serene, and never again having any problems. The first thing I learned was that not only was it not necessary to love everybody, but that doing so would likely give me a permanent mental cramp. Purple dinosaurs love everybody. Humans are sometimes indifferent, sometimes they dislike, and sometimes they even hate, if they're healthy.

The permanent blessing of serenity was another fiction that was dispelled when NA came out with its keytags to recognize various lengths of clean time. On one side is the NA symbol; on the other, "Clean and Serene" and then the number of days, months, etc. Every group I know of takes the word "clean" very seriously. "Serene" is not taken quite so seriously, since we are all still searching for that person who has managed to hammer together thirty straight days of serenity.

Problems. Life is problems, and some of those problems, such as the death of a loved one, working through old issues, confronting a child who is on drugs, squaring things away with the law, getting divorced, are serenity-smashers. Recovery is not a state of grace within which the recovered have achieved celestial sainthood, drifting from cloud to cloud, wringing wet with bliss. Recovery means not using and becoming a full human being complete with the tools to deal with the problems of living life on life's terms, and every now and then you step in some dog crap.

My heroes in the program, now, are not those who look good and sound as though they have a corner on the wisdom and serenity markets. My heroes are those who have spine-crushing problems and continue, one day at a time, to learn how to deal with those problems without using.

27. The Impossible Dream

The primary symptom of this disease is the incredible, exhausting, and never-ending effort to get sick, stay sick, and get ever sicker. One of the dragon's most effective weapons in this enterprise is perfectionism, which is an attitude that sets impossibly high standards and is displeased with anything less. It is a setup for failure. The only thing perfect about perfectionism is that it makes a perfectly logical, if completely bogus, argument for going back to using.

"I cannot stay clean if such-and-such is not perfect. Such-and-such will always have flaws. Hence, I cannot stay clean."

The perfection bug is usually not that honest about itself. Instead it hides itself behind "shoulds," "oughts," "I wants," and "I needs."

In rehab I heard an addict say, "But I don't want to go to meetings. I'm a busy person with family obligations. Besides, who wants to associate with a bunch of losers?"

Someone in the group answered, "Recovery doesn't have a damned thing to do with what you want; only with what you need."

28. Perfecting Perfectionism

A few years ago I took up alpine skiing. One day as I was at the outside racks preparing to ski down to the chair lift, I saw a strange thing. A man about my age standing a few feet from me, for no apparent reason, fell down on the snow. He was in the process of getting up when I asked, "Are you okay?"

"Sure," he answered. "I do that every day before I hit the slopes so I can enjoy skiing. Now I don't have to worry about falling down and ending some kind of perfect performance. The performance is already over."

Perhaps it takes a recovering addict to see the great wisdom in this, and in another fellow. When he buys a new car, the first thing he does upon delivery is take his new key and put a scratch in the fender's gleaming finish. "Now all I have to do is enjoy driving instead of worrying about when I'm going to get that first scratch."

Today I'll try to keep in mind that the one guaranteed way to make my day imperfect is to try and make it perfect.

29. The Higher Power Thing

"I can't accept this higher power crap. Religion is bullshit." At a meeting all we have to do is hear that and all of the hard cases smile. We've all been there, god-killers and fanatics both. Someone will usually point out that the program has nothing to do with religion. It is, instead, a spiritual program.

"What's the difference?" the hard case will ask.

One answer was that "Religion is organization; spirituality is power." Another way I heard it was this: "Religion is for those who don't want to go to Hell. Spirituality is for those who have been to Hell and don't want to go back."

30. You'll Grow into It

Early in the program an old-timer took me aside, sat me down in front of a pencil and a piece of paper, and said, "Okay, design yourself a higher power. The first thing you need to give your higher power is the power to keep you clean." I wrote that down and have been adding things ever since. I am an individual in an individual program. I needed an individually tailored higher power, not one off the rack.

How can this be? Isn't there but one truth? How can anything good come from a collection of different higher powers? With one truth, doesn't that make all the other powers false?

Speaking only for myself (and about a hundred addicts I know), truth is a lot bigger than most folks imagine. Whatever it is that we are tapped into for power to recover is so large, so complex, and so powerful that it can fill any bill of particulars you require. Male, female, neuter, corporeal existence, vaporous, humanish, alien, a mountain, ocean, or flower—it can become any and all of these things. However you define it, it will work.

"You mean, I'm supposed to sit here and create God?" I asked. "That's stupid. How can I believe in something like that?"

"No one said you have to believe in it," answered the old-timer. "All you have to do is do it."

31. The Gods Do Not Claim the Jerks Who Use Their Names

There are the nonbelievers:

"Okay, I've picked a higher power, but I'll be damned if I'll believe in it," declared one hard case to his sponsor.

"That's okay," said the old-timer, "just as long as it believes in you."

—◆—

And there are the super-true-believers, recognized by the blue flames they have shooting from their asses:

> *"This stuff about all paths lead to God is just another way to avoid doing anything," said the self-ordained blue flamer. "If you are serious about getting a higher power, forget about all this design-your-own-supreme-being nonsense. The only god is a god of God's understanding, not yours."*

It is often difficult to know what to do with a blue flamer on full afterburners. Everyone is exactly where they're supposed to be, and using addicts stoned out of their gourds have said and done things in meetings that have helped me. Still, orthodox scripture hawks and fundamentalist Jesus jammers often sound to newcomers as though they speak for the program. "This is who you must pray to and how you must do it if you want to recover . . . " and so on.

If I had been presented with such a blue light at my first program meeting, I doubt if I would have ever made it to a second. There is one truth every newcomer carries into every kind of Twelve Step program: "I don't *have* to do anything."

That's why the Steps are a "suggested program of recovery," not commandments. That's why it's a "God of our understanding," not a particular being, discipline, or organization. To recover, the newcomer is going to have to find a source of strength and help that will work for that newcomer, not one that works for the tolerance-challenged.

When one of these carriers of the light and truth hits a meeting, there are usually a lot of things running around in my skull I could say that would make the point in the most destructive manner possible. What keeps these little gems from running out on my tongue is that religious nuts need recovery too. All I can do is talk about the "God of our understanding" provisions in the Steps and share what works for me. Then, after the meeting, I call my sponsor and fill *his* ear with all of the nasty things I wanted to say.

—◆—

It is a spiritual, not a religious, program. It is also not an evangelical program. My higher power is mine. It is only as I understand it. My HP needs no one else's approval or understanding. In addition, everyone else has a higher power of their own, whether they know it or not, and no one needs me to shove my version down their throat.

32. Exercises, Exercises

A young woman was sharing at a meeting one night, and I was astounded at what she said. She was absolutely beautiful, inside and out. She thought she was ugly, stupid, and unlovable. One half of my head yelled at the other half of my head, "She's not unlovable; she's crazy!"

I loved her and everybody I knew in the program loved her, but there she was, feeling about herself the way I've always felt about myself. Was it possible that I was lovable and didn't know it? It was very confusing.

"Emotions are like muscles," said someone at another meeting. "The ones that get the most exercise are the strongest." I learned this for a fact when I tried out the "You're okay" mirror affirmation described in "Rozanne's Story" in *Overeaters Anonymous*. It's nothing more than looking in the mirror once a day for six months and saying to yourself, "You're okay." No fair making faces or raspberries. You look at that face in the mirror and say, "You're okay."

The first time I tried the mirror affirmation, I discovered something very disturbing. I found out what it was that I said to myself every time I caught sight of myself in a mirror. I'd say, "Hi, asshole." That particular feeling didn't need any more exercise, so I stopped doing that. Then, once a day, I would look into the mirror and say to myself, "You're okay." After thirty days of this, I stopped what I decided was a waste of time. However, about a week later I was passing by that same mirror and caught a glimpse of myself. At the same time a sudden realization thundered into my head. "You really *are* okay!" I said out loud. I felt it, too.

Today I want to remember to tell myself that I'm okay. I don't want the fact that I'm worth recovery to slip my mind.

33. What's Love Got to Do with It?

One night at a meeting I was feeling particularly loathsome toward myself. My focus was square on everything within myself that I considered a flaw, which seemed to be an awfully big target right then. The dragon had me by the heart, and I was well down the self-pity chute. That was when someone I knew at the meeting said, "We love you, Barry, lots and lots and lots."

The next meeting I attended he was there again and did the same thing. Every time I began verbally beating myself up, he'd say "We love you, Barry, lots and lots and lots." What was worse, others at the meeting began picking it up. The most comfortable way for me to regard this was as a joke. But I couldn't keep it in that pigeonhole for long. Almost every time I'd get a hug from someone in the program, I'd hear, "I love you." It was coming from everywhere.

Could they all be fools? Losers? Liars? Could they all be trying to pull a con on me? I had to look hard at those who were telling me that they loved me. I was forced to admit that at least some of them had to be sincere. Then I looked at myself to see if there was anything in there worth loving. I found a thing here, a thing there, and then a flood of things about myself worth loving. That was when I could begin to take those first few hesitant steps toward loving myself. What my friends did was very simple: they loved me until I could love myself and then love them back.

A year later, the man who started the "I love you, lots and lots and lots" business was diagnosed with terminal brain tumors and lung cancer. It wasn't a pretty way to go, and those of us in the program were his pall bearers when it came time to bury him two months later. Before he died, however, I had several chances to visit him in the hospital and at his home, where he eventually passed away. On all of those occasions I got to take that wasted body in my arms and tell him that I loved him. He would tell me that he loved me, and I could take it in. I can't think of a greater gift to leave to anyone.

Today I can remember that I am worth loving, which means there is no limit on who I can love or who can love me. I also remember that it is an action program. I can only learn to love myself by loving myself, which is okay. After all, beating myself up never was part of the program.

34. Minding the View

A person was sharing at a meeting, and nothing seemed to be going right with her life. All she seemed to be able to focus on were flaws, mistakes, and losses. She couldn't stand the men and women with whom she worked, her love relationship was aground, and there seemed to be no point in going on. When she was finished another woman leaned forward and said, "It sounds as though you might have a bad case of *octal rectalitis.*"

"What's that?"

"*Octal rectalitis.* That's looking at the world through your asshole."

—◆—

Negativity is often described as a person looking upon a half-filled glass as half-empty rather than half-full. That doesn't even scratch the surface of the truly negative. An addict with a genuinely vicious dragon on his back can look at that half-empty glass and see the fingerprints and watermarks on it, can wrinkle his nose at the remaining contents as probably being spoiled, and will probably project how he'll cut his lip on the edge of the glass should he attempt to take a sip of the poisonous contents. *Octal rectalitis.* It's a view of reality filtered by the dragon.

The cure for this terrible malady is not to take on a perfectly positive view of everything. This everything-is-perfect-in-my-life view is a disease called *octal rosiosy*. That's looking through rose-colored glasses at the gates of Disneyland. It's sort of like singing, spreading rose petals, and skipping through a minefield. Sooner or later the reality bill will come due.

For most of us the safe path is balance. Today I try to remember that when things look the worst, I need to check the eyepiece through which I'm looking. If I'm having an attack of O.R., it's time to reach for my gratitude list, reach for the phone, and head to a meeting.

35. Recovery Commandos

A woman shared about how she began to be troubled by a few little things, a few little problems, that she thought she really needed to handle on her own. They were private things, a bit embarrassing, and really no big deal. She began by not talking about the problems, and she continued by cutting down on meetings and isolating herself from her sponsor and others in the program. Using only the contents of her own head she found the answers her dragon was looking for. That she made it back to the program without using made her one of the lucky ones.

"I've given up being a recovery commando. If addiction was a problem I could handle by myself I would have handled it years ago." I've heard this at meetings and I try to remember it every time I find myself tempted to boogie with my disease. Often, however, the dragon leaves me with a very selective memory. It's important for me to remember that there is no problem I have that cannot be cut down to size by sharing it with someone else in the program. At a meeting, over the phone, together over a cup of decaf, the problems get cut in half and the joys become doubled. When I share, more often than not I find that the thing that's deviling me is really a nonproblem. As an old-timer once said, "I'm an old man. I've lived a long time and had many problems, most of which never happened."

36. You Can Never Tell Who Is Awake

At one meeting a returnee back from the nightmare was sharing his reasons for not calling his sponsor. "I woke up at three in the morning," he said, "and my head was spinning. I couldn't get back to sleep so I stayed up thinking. I didn't want to wake up my sponsor, so I kept on thinking and stewing on a few setbacks I've had, and the next thing I knew I was out there drinking."

Several of us glanced at the guy's sponsor, expecting a blast from that direction, but the man did nothing but sit there, his face without expression. A couple nights later at another meeting the returnee shared again. He said, "The night I came back and told about my slip, the guilt was washed away and I was feeling great. I went to bed that night and slept as solid as a rock. Then the phone rang. I woke up out of a sound sleep, looked at the clock, and saw it was three in the morning. Figuring it was an emergency, I answered the phone. It was my sponsor. He said, 'I just wanted to let you know that I'm up.' Then the sonofabitch hung up on me!"

—◆—

For today I need to remember that an addict inside his own head is behind enemy lines. The way to safety is to reach out *when* I need to reach out. There's not much point in taking vitamins after the funeral.

37. What's in a Name?

When I first came into the program, I identified myself at rehab meetings as an alcoholic. After I got honest about the prescription drugs I had been using, I amended my identification to alcoholic and drug addict. After adding compulsive overeating, compulsive gambling, codependency, and so on to my list, it was getting to where I was taking up a good portion of each meeting just identifying myself. Because of this, on occasion I would introduce myself as a "Renaissance compulsive—I do it all." Finally, since every substance and behavior I was struggling with was an addiction, I shortened it all down to "addict" and left it at that.

It was rare, but every now and then someone who wasn't pleased with how I was identifying myself would point out what I should call myself in *his* particular program meetings. I read the rules for all of the Twelve Step programs I've ever been in, and every single one of them has the same qualification for membership listed under the Third Tradition: "The only requirement for membership is a desire to stop [drinking, using, eating compulsively, etc.]." I have yet to find a rule that says I even have to talk at a meeting, much less what I have to call myself.

What someone else chooses to use for an identification is none of my business. What I call myself is me admitting to having this disease, and it is no one else's business. There was one fellow who used to run around meetings like a sheep dog, barking at anyone who appeared to be straying from the flock. I heard his sponsor practically command him to tattoo the Third Tradition on the insides of his eyelids and to remember that it's an individual program and everyone is exactly where they're supposed to be: "Just as the Twelve Steps are there to help us recover from the disease, the Twelve Traditions are there to protect the program from us."

38. I Gotta Do *What*?

A few years ago someone from "on high" required everyone in our program's meetings to identify themselves with a particular label. For the next three months at meetings, consequently, I defiantly identified myself as a "compulsive orangutan banger." I even had a qualification that began: "When I first started out, I was just monkeying around; then I went ape!" In the same spirit, a politically correct program sister referred to herself as "chemically challenged." After a while we remembered the Third Tradition, made a copy of it, and sent it to World Service. Then we all calmed down.

For today I remember that my recovery, and only *my* recovery, is my responsibility. It is mine, however, and no program officer has any authority to dictate anything. I must remember as well that everyone is exactly where he or she is supposed to be, and if I cannot accept that, I can always start another meeting. As they say, all you need to start a new meeting is a resentment, a coffeepot, and a place to plug it in.

39. Getting Up with Fleas

Early on in recovery we are advised to "Stick with the winners." Of course, as a compulsive gambler, my reaction to this advice was, "All right! I can do that. Just show me a winner."

In Gamblers Anonymous it is sometimes said, "No one quits winners," meaning that compulsive gamblers who are deliriously happy because they are winning money by the barge load, and their family, friends, and employers are showering them with love and praise, don't often find themselves at a GA meeting. We only make it through the doors when the consequences of not going through those doors exceeds bearable pain limits. When the job is gone, the family is gone or threatening to go, the health is shot, the debts have climbed into the stratosphere, and suicide is looking more and more like a viable world plan, then a GA meeting might not look so bad. It's the same in all Twelve Step programs. We have to lose the glitter outside before we can see the light from the other side of the door.

It seems as though we have to be losers before we can become winners. We get to be winners by sticking with the winners, and who are they? Who do we pick for sponsors? Who do we hang out with outside meetings? Who do we listen to inside meetings? Our choices select for us the kind and quality of example, experience, support, and maturity that we make available to our own recoveries.

There is no perfect or risk-free way to do it. I find someone who has something I want and then I go to that person and ask for help. I also keep in mind that no one is perfect. That includes both my choices and the objects of my choices. For the good choices I make, I am grateful. The not-so-good choices I call experience.

—◆—

It is said that it takes good judgment to avoid mistakes, it takes experience to develop good judgment, and it takes mistakes to gain experience. When I am being especially kind to myself I listen to those who have already made the mistakes for me.

40. Willingness to Be Willing

The subject at the Adult Children of Alcoholics meeting was forgiveness, and one young man was sharing about forgiving his parents. At that precise moment my entire head shut down. "Forgive?" I thought. "My parents? Are you insane? Personally, I hope they're both roasting in Hell over a slow fire!"

I had been gypped out of a childhood, out of my innocence, out of my health, out of a family, and out of a couple of parents. Before I was going to consider anything like forgiveness, I wanted to see something put down on this colossal debt.

That night, my head burning into my pillow, it was getting very clear to me how much brain space and energy this matter was using. It was square in the way of my serenity. That was when it got through to me that forgiveness isn't letting someone else off the hook. It isn't something we do for others. Forgiveness is something we do for ourselves.

Muttering to myself, I got out of bed, went into the living room, and sat there in the dark contemplating forgiveness. At meetings they told me how to do it. "Pray for them," someone suggested.

My immediate response had been to say, "Dear God, I pray that these bastards get exactly what they have coming to them."

"I don't think you quite have the hang of it," my sponsor observed.

At another meeting I heard someone give the think-and-do version of forgiveness. "Pray for them by asking your HP to grant them everything you pray to get for yourself."

I couldn't bring myself to do it. I wanted so badly to put all this behind me, but it seemed like the crimes against me were simply too huge.

I had heard at a meeting that, if you can't pray to forgive, pray for the willingness to forgive. I tried that, but it was still too much for me to carry. What I could do, though, was to pray for the willingness to have the willingness. Then I went back to bed and tried to put the whole thing out of my mind.

Three weeks later at another ACA meeting, the subject was once again forgiveness. I was suddenly thunderstruck by the feelings I had. The resentments against my parents were gone. Somehow, without me being conscious of the change, I had let go of the blame, the hate, the pain, and the constant reliving of this agony we call resentment. Asking for the willingness to have the willingness brought me to and through forgiveness.

Today if I can't forgive, I ask for the willingness. If I can't ask for the willingness, I ask for the willingness to have the willingness. I do only what I can do and my higher power handles the rest.

41. White Flag Time

We had heard it all before. She had given up substances and went to meetings, but had made no other changes. She was doing it her way and was constantly running into herself. "It's such a struggle for me," she shared at a meeting. "Drugs are all around me, the craving doesn't lighten up for a second, there are so many pressures on me, obligations, people pulling me in a hundred directions, it's a fight. Every day I wake up in a war zone. With all that I'm doing, when is it going to get better?"

"See How Hard I Try," said another addict. "That's 'shit' spelled with two Hs."

"The secret to winning your war," said an old-timer, "is to surrender."

"Surrender" to most of us sounds like losing, failure, defeat, coming in last. Many of us, in the past, surrendered to the disease. I remember very clearly the day I stood in front of the bathroom mirror and realized that I could not possibly survive without those damned pills. There was that and alcohol, too. I looked at my face and said, "I guess this is just one more thing I have to put up with."

It was such an extreme moment of humiliation and despair, that I never wanted to face anything like it ever again. If I was going to recover I was going to have to fight. More than that, I had to win. Then I would be told about the double-h shit and the need to surrender. This time, however, the surrender is to recovery, not to the disease.

In the program sense, surrender means to relinquish control. For years, completely in control, my life was a blazing disaster. I let go a little when I agreed to go to rehab, even though the only reason I went was that I figured with all those addicts out there I ought to be able to work up a pretty good poker game. I turned a little more control over to the rehab when I agreed to stay, even though gambling was forbidden.

After rehab, I loosened my grasp a bit more when I attended meetings, turning at least that small amount of my time and control over to the program. When I got a sponsor (one I would use), when I asked a higher power for help, when I picked up the phone—every time I asked for help—I surrendered a little more. The more complete the surrender, the better things became.

Whenever I find myself in a battle, I try to remember it's because I haven't surrendered. To surrender I need to turn the control of my recovery over to those who can make that recovery possible: my program family and my higher power.

42. How to Lose Thirty Ugly Pounds

In some OA groups they refer to those who focus on losses, might-have-beens, and all of the other rough spots of human existence as "waste watchers."

"Look at this! Look at that! How can I possibly go on?" wails the waste watcher, the dragon grinning through the smoke. "This is wrong, that's wrong, this is unfair, that's terribly unjust, this disease shouldn't have happened to me. Why me?"

If a certain program member is in the room, chances are she'll ask, "Would you like to lose thirty ugly pounds?"

"Sure," the waste watcher will answer. "What should I do?"

"Change your attitude."

43. The Call of the Dark Side

Our disease feeds off loss and disaster and uses them as excuses to use, whether that using is with food, drugs, relationships, exercise, work, or whatever. When the dragon is in full control, nothing comes between the addict and the object of the addiction. If we need to generate excuses to use, the dragon adjusts our focus. If that isn't sufficient, we will be urged to sabotage ourselves to the point where we can say with genuine sincerity, "If you had my troubles, you'd use, too."

When we become abstinent from our addictive behavior, this does not change how we look at things. Changing how we see things is an active process that takes time and effort. Even when we are looking at things realistically, no one is exempt from having his or her focus go out of whack on occasion.

It has been said that we all have everything we need to be happy in this very moment. The hard case, however, has a long way to go to get where he or she already is. It always depends on the map we use and how we see it.

—◆—

For today I will try to look at things for what they are, accepting the things I cannot change, asking for the courage to change the things I can, remembering that the only thing I really need to do to be happy is be happy. As an anonymous poet once penned:

> *See the happy moron,*
> *He doesn't give a damn.*
> *I wish I were a moron—*
> *My God, perhaps I am!*

44. Mix and Match

Early recovery is confusing enough without throwing an unwise and unintentional love relationship on top of it. Accordingly, when the subject of getting a sponsor comes up, old-timers will mention that it is recommended that men have male sponsors and women have female sponsors. The exceptions to this recommendation, of course, refer to gays and lesbians. Here males and females may team up, but only if *both* are homosexual.

There was a young man a few years ago, fresh out of rehab, who chose a lesbian for his sponsor, knowing full well that she was a lesbian when he asked her.

Since there was no possibility of a love interest on her part with the man, she agreed.

Only one problem. He fell madly and hopelessly in love with her. He shared this, his pain and frustration, at a meeting, and shared as well how he was right up against going back out and using. For once, no one suggested to him that he call his sponsor. One old-timer, however, did make an observation. He was shaking his head in awe and admiration when he said, "This is better than sitting on a branch and sawing it off at the trunk. What an absolutely magnificent setup. Unless you can turn it around, there is no possible way for you not to fail. She can't return your love, there is no way for you to express yours, you can't live sober without her, and you have to go down. The dragon scores another one."

It was suggested to him that he get another sponsor. When she found out about how he felt, his sponsor did fire him, again with the suggestion that he get a male sponsor. He didn't. Instead he pined away for about two days then picked up a bottle and dropped back into the nightmare. As we learn the hard way, recovery's not for everyone.

This is why, when the subject of sponsors comes up at meetings, the recommendation is still hetero men to hetero men, hetero women to hetero women, gay men to lesbian women, and vice versa. Beware of any combination that can be a setup for failure. Of course, one night after an old-timer illustrated the recommendation by sharing his own ordeal, someone asked, "Well, what about bisexuals?"

The old-timer's eyes crossed a bit, then he said, "I don't know. I've never run into the situation. When I do, and I'm confident that day is coming soon, I'm certain the answer will be revealed to me. Smart ass."

—◆—

At another meeting, a man shared another piece of sponsorship wisdom: "My wife and I both came into the program at the same time and we decided to sponsor each other. It worked great until I did my Fifth Step with her. She filed for divorce the next day."

An additional piece of wisdom was dropped after a meeting when a newcomer asked, "Well, what about just sponsoring myself?"

Before any of us could begin listing all of the reasons why such an arrangement would be useless to his recovery, a passing old-timer said, "If you sponsor yourself, your sponsor is an asshole."

—◆—

For today I'll remember to put my pride aside and take into account the experiences of those in my program family. I want to recover, and to do that I have to be teachable.

45. Keeping the Miracle Working

The First Tradition says, "Our common welfare should come first; personal recovery depends upon program unity."

"Understanding the First Tradition is easy," said an old-timer. "Without the program, we're dead. Living by the First Tradition is simple, too. We ask ourselves if what we're doing is killing us or helping us to stay alive."

The Twelve Steps show us how to live with ourselves. The Twelve Traditions show us how to live with each other, which is no mean trick in a society made up of compulsive control freaks, compliant people-pleasers, mistrustful paranoids, and convoluted nitpickers in various stages of recovery. In any setting other than the program it would probably mean war. That we can work together for our common welfare is part of the recovery miracle.

Our common welfare is nothing more than keeping the miracle working for us and for whoever wants it. It's keeping the meetings going, making and keeping the help available, carrying the message to those who still suffer. Sometimes, however, caught up in the moment during a sharing session or at a business meeting, it's easy to put egos before our mutual recovery. For example, if a group guru or program officer at a meeting objects to something by becoming offensive or aggressive, our common welfare is no longer first. "I'm right and you're wrong" has replaced it. Injuries happen, feelings become hurt, the meeting becomes less a haven of love and support and more a place to fuel resentments. And if our mutual recovery is no longer the most important thing, can relapse be far behind?

In NA's preamble to the Twelve Traditions it says, "As long as the ties that bind us together are stronger than those that would tear us apart, all will be well." For today I'll remember to ask myself which kind of ties I'm fabricating by my actions. If I find my pride, fear, or need to control coming before our common welfare, it's time for me to get an attitude transplant and rethink my priorities.

46. Born Again—*Ouch*!

"I suppose growing up isn't ever easy, but doing it at the age of forty is the pits."

I listened to my program friend and I could relate. Everything that I used to handle by escaping into numbness was now something that had to be dealt with by doing it, and I had none of the skills. Angry people scared me, and my reaction was to either cower or explode in their faces.

Thinking of some of the temper tantrums and rage stages I'd been through, and had put others through, was enough to make me blush. One time someone cut me off in traffic and I went berserk, forgetting everything that I had ever learned about acceptance, patience, self-worth; that I was in my second year of recovery, and that lives were at stake. The only thing I seemed to be able to focus on was running that bastard off the road. There was a chase, some close calls, but thanks to some belated sanity, I called it off.

There are times when I am driving, shopping, going to a movie, or eating in a restaurant when I look around me and wonder how fast the place would clear out if those around me could see into my head for just a moment. The craziness of being fifteen years old in the body of a fifty-year-old often makes me leery of sharing with others. When I do share, however, I find that I am not alone.

We all stopped growing emotionally the moment we started using addictively, whatever the addiction. The first time we handled a loss or disappointment by drinking, shooting, popping, eating, climbing into bed with someone, or filling our minds with work, games, or religion, we stopped living in the real world and began living in a fantasy land where problems are supposed to take care of themselves. Growing up involves changing my address from fantasy land to Planet Earth.

Yet it often leaves us thinking that the problems of the world were just waiting for us to stop using so that they could all jump us at the same time. How many times have I heard, and said, "Every time I struggle to my feet I seem to get slapped down again. What am I supposed to be doing?"

Someone will say, "Don't use, go to meetings, and ask for help."

"Yeah, I know," someone once responded, "HP doesn't give me any more than I can handle in one day, although I think he might want to check my load limit specs once in a while. I think HP has me mixed up with King Kong."

It has been said that recovery is like being born again, as an adult. If it were easy, everybody would be doing it. Today, instead of escaping from reality, I'll take reality as it comes and get the help I need to deal with it.

47. Hanging on to Experience

A woman at a meeting asked for some feedback. "They say to forgive and forget, but I just can't forget what's happened."

"That's good," said one of the addicts. "Not learning from the mistakes of others is prideful. Not learning from your own mistakes is insanity."

Resentment is the main rut of what's called "stinkin' thinkin.'" Forgiveness is the way out of that rut. Forgetting is the direct route right back into that rut. Said an old-timer, "A cat who sits on a hot stove and burns its ass doesn't spend the rest of its life resenting the stove. It lets go of the resentment, but not the experience. It's not going to sit on that hot stove again."

Of course, some of us have known some stupid cats, but the point is nonetheless important.

There was a young man who wandered in and out of the program dozens of times from when he was fifteen until he was in his twenties. For a while I was his sponsor, and even lent him money for food, which he promptly went out and spent on drugs. By the next year he was back in the program and was in a bind with his landlord for back rent. I had forgiven and forgotten the previous experience, and lent him money once again. Would you believe he took that money and spent it on drugs?

Psychiatrist Thomas Szasz wrote, "The stupid neither forgive nor forget; the naive forgive and forget; the wise forgive but do not forget." Forgiveness is letting go of resentment. Forgetting is letting go of experience. Experience is the foundation of good judgment, and good judgment is what I need for my recovery and to be of help to others. For today I can let go of the resentment, but hang on to what I have learned.

48. The Collector

Marcus Aurelius wrote, "Look beneath the surface; let not the several quality of a thing nor its worth escape thee."

—◆—

It seems strange that to begin recovery we must feel as though we are worth recovery. Yet it seems to take the entire recovery process to reach the stage where we think we are worth anything. It is a paradox that can be answered only by acting "as if." Act as if I'm worth recovery, even though I don't feel like I'm worth anything, in the hopes that someday the feelings will catch up. To me it seemed like therapy through hypocrisy.

Waiting for those feelings to catch up sometimes seems like it will take forever. Nevertheless, they do catch up. Often it only takes looking at the same old thing from a new angle.

One of the lowest points in a friend's recovery was when he finally got honest with himself about being a compulsive gambler. "I was already in AA and Al-Anon, ACA, NA, and OA. And now this! It seemed like I was some kind of perverted collector gathering all of the Twelve Step programs I could. I felt like a freak; not even worth the space that I was taking up."

Sometime later, at an Al-Anon meeting, a young man there asked him to be his sponsor. The program collector was totally floored by what seemed to be a really sick suggestion. He asked the young man if he was sure he wanted him for a sponsor. Before he could answer, the collector began going through his list of addictions and afflictions, but the young man interrupted him. "I've heard your story before," he said. "That's why I want you to be my sponsor. You've been to a lot of places I don't want to go."

"And there it was," said the collector. "All of a sudden I was no longer one of God's sick jokes. Instead, I was *qualified.*"

49. What's Important?

There was a woman in NA who had a leg amputated because of complications associated with diabetes and cancer. "The pain was terrible, and it all got mixed up with the drugs they gave me for the pain. I became addicted all over again, and it wasn't until I was detoxed that I had any feelings about myself, and what I felt wasn't good. Even though I had no choice, I was ashamed of having taken the drugs, and I was even more ashamed of becoming addicted again. Most of all, I was ashamed of losing my leg. I was even ashamed that I was ashamed. The amputation made me a freak, something to make jokes about, something less than human. I was on the edge of that big old canyon full of self-pity and dived right in with no intention of ever coming up. How could someone as useless and worthless as I was be allowed to live? Why would anyone want to?

"Then, shortly after my physical therapy began, my doctor asked me if I would talk to a young patient of his who had just had his leg removed. 'Should I bring my own razor blades?' I asked. The doctor thought I was joking.

"I had no idea what I had to offer, but I agreed. I rolled myself into his room and talked to him, shared with him what it had been like for me, how angry I still was, and the work I was doing to recover. To my astonishment, it helped him. To my even greater surprise, it turned my own life around. It's just like how it works in the program: one addict helping another. This didn't happen to me because I was worthless, and this happening to me didn't make me worthless. In fact, it added to how I can be of help to others. It made me worth more. And everyone could see it except me."

One of many program miracles is discovering the "practicing these principles in all our affairs," part of Step Twelve. It's not just recovery; it's a whole new way of life.

—◆—

50. Beauty Scars

When I first came into the program, I found it almost impossible to use the telephone to ask for help. Once, when I had to make a call for business reasons, I took the opportunity to unload on the associate I called, even though he was not in the program and his main life problem was finding matching covers for his new golf clubs. After I finished talking about the things that were bothering me, there was a stunned silence on the other end of the line. When he at last spoke he provided me with this choice piece of feedback: "Damn, Barry, I don't know how you can stay sober."

—◆—

There are times when I wonder of what possible use to me a person who had never had any problems could be. Perhaps as a scientific curiosity. I always imagine that such a person would probably look like the Pillsbury doughboy. His big trauma is being poked in the middle until he giggles. What would be the point in sharing my nightmares with such a being? A person who has never had any problems is a person who has no experience, nothing to overcome, nothing to share. Every hit we have taken during our lives, every disappointment, depression, disaster, disease, and crisis has added to our experience. They have brought us to where we are today, and where we are today is in a position to share our experiences with others.

Right now I can share with those who are going through the same things that I've gone through to let them know recovery is possible and that they are not alone. For things that are a matter of choice, I can share with those who haven't yet started to let them know the consequences. My scars, both external and internal, are marks of my passage through life, signs of what I've learned, and reminders of what I can pass onto others. I am worth the space I take up on this planet. Today I will act as if, knowing that, sooner or later, my feelings will catch up.

51. Pushing the River

"Everyone grows at his or her own pace," we hear at meetings. Still, now and then I feel like demanding, "I want patience *now*! I want that peace of mind, I want serenity and contentment, I want to feel good about myself and have the courage to stand up for myself. I want to lay the past to rest and stop trembling in fear about the future. And I'm sick and tired of screwing around waiting for it. I'd be patient, but it takes too damned long! I want what I want when I want it!"

Then I might hear someone say, "A ten-mile walk into the woods is a ten-mile walk back out."

Another might say, "It takes time, and TIME stands for This I Must Earn."

Still another might say, "The way I heard it was, This I Must Excrete."

Sometimes I will see how someone in the program has handled a difficult situation with courage, brilliance, and serenity, and begin beating myself up with "When am I going to be able to do that?"

Just about then some old-timer will say, "You can't push the river. All you can do is go with the flow."

— ◆ —

Willpower, determination, and bulling my way through seemed like the only ways to accomplish things before I came into the program. In recovery, however, I'm told that willpower and determination are useless and that bulling my way through won't achieve anything lasting except unhappiness. My task now is to turn it over and let the program work for me. Do the footwork and let the destination take care of itself. "Okay, but to find serenity, what am I supposed to *do*?"

"Work the Twelve Steps, go to meetings, and ask for help," someone will invariably say. Once, when I was in a feverish search for a higher power, I read a Hindu prescription for reaching ultimate truth from the *Bhagavad Gita*. It advised me "Do your duty, always; but without attachment." I took that to mean doing what I needed to do for me, unattached to outcomes. In other words, walk the walk and focus on the present moment. The first real meditation I ever did was on that line, and it still lets me visit serenity when I do what it advises.

One time at a meeting an anonymous visitor shared with us a little piece of poetry he called "The Enigma of Peace and Meaning." It went like this:

> *The solution*
> *Is to share the solution,*
> *And to live life as though*
> *The only thing you can share*
> *Is to say,*
> *"Do as I do."*

— ◆ —

For now I'll walk the walk and keep my attention on the now, secure in the knowledge that the gifts of the program will come to me, not necessarily when I want, but when I am ready.

52. Not Screaming Is a Good Sign

Step Two: "We came to believe that a power greater than ourselves could restore us to sanity."

— ◆ —

At a meeting we heard, "I was working on Step Two with a sponsee, when he asked me what sanity is. The way he put it, he wasn't sure he wanted to be restored to some higher power's idea of sanity, which might be anything down to and including shaving his head and handing out flowers at the airport. Before he goes for it, he said, he wants to know what it is. I could use some help on this: what is sanity?"

Answered an old-timer, "Not screaming is a good sign." What followed after that was a list of things that sanity was not. Not being in jail is one sign. Not waking up in a gutter is another. Not ranting or raving. Not nagging or caretaking. Not beating the crap out of strangers, friends, and loved ones. Not beating the crap out of yourself. And there were more symptoms of sanity: not cutting yourself with razors; not being obsessed with others, drugs, food, sex, gambling, violence, suicide, or anything else; not damning God when you wake up in the morning; not being constantly confused yet convinced you have all the answers; not needing to be right all the time; not needing to be in control of others all of the time, and so on, through a list of the million and one crazy things all of us have done and have related and related to at meetings.

All of these things, however, are what sanity is *not*. The sponsee's question had to do with what sanity *is*. The dictionary says that sanity is the condition of sound mental health, but what is that? Few of us had any experience with this uncommon abnormality. Of the times in the past when I thought I was sane, I was either high, emotionally shut down, or in deep denial. Specifically, what is being sane?

The folks at the meeting tried out a few things: peace of mind, serenity, contentment, being able to love, being able to be loved, being able to tell the difference between what's bad for me and what's good for me *and* having the love for myself necessary to pick the good over the bad, the ability and the courage to feel all of my feelings. It seemed that this thing called sanity had no simple definition that had any direct meaning. My sanity would be something drawn from my experiences, tailored to my individuality, and specific to me and what I needed to overcome and become. As we were contemplating all of these heavy thoughts, another old-timer put things into focus by keeping it simple.

"It sounds like your sponsee's already done a good job on Step Two. He already believes that a power greater than himself can restore him to sanity. He just doesn't know what sanity is. He's looking for HP's menu on sanity to see if that's what he wants, and that's part of making up your mind in Step Three: 'Made a decision to turn our will and our lives over to the care of God *as we understood him.*'"

For myself, I want this sanity even though I'm not really certain what it is or where it will bring me. I remember what I was and where I was before the program, and whatever and wherever sanity is, it's got to be an improvement. I also believe a power greater than myself can do this. I see the miracles all about me every time I go to a meeting.

53. How Bad Does It Have to Get?

Although creaking and bent with age, there is a joke that is still told around program coffeepots, which shows its truth. Two women are standing by the side of a grave, and one of the women, the spouse of the deceased, says, "It was just terrible. Just like he did every night, he got drunk and went into his workshop and turned on all of his power tools. Usually he'd just drink and then nip off a finger or toe, cut off an ear, or put out an eye. Once he got drunk and cut off a hand. Once on a real bad drunk a year later he cut off his leg. This last time he got drunk he cut off his head and there wasn't anything they could do about that."

Her friend nodded in sympathy. "An alcoholic, was he?" she asked.

The wife of the deceased opened her eyes wide in horror and shook her head. "Oh, no!" she answered. "He wasn't *that* bad!"

— ◆ —

That old Egyptian river, denial, is the relapse demon's main tool. Denial can blind the addict and everyone close to the addict. As long as we cannot see, we cannot turn when we come to the edge of that cliff—not unless someone warns us *and we listen to the warning*.

There was a fellow who shared that his therapist and his sponsor both had suggested he get into a twenty-eight-day treatment program. He asked the meeting for some feedback on what he should do. A number of us shared our rehab experiences, and all of us who knew him urged him to go. He definitely needed some time away from the scene to put together the skills necessary to stay clean.

He was reluctant, however. There was the time, the expense, a few things he really needed to deal with on his own, this, and that. He did, however, thank everyone for their input. Two weeks later he got drunk and was beaten to death in a bar.

—◆—

It has been said many times: "If addiction was a problem I could have handled by myself, I would have done so many years ago." If the main tool of relapse is the closed-mindedness of denial, the main tool of recovery is the open-mindedness of fellowship: addicts helping other addicts to see what needs to be seen to recover. The millions of us who suffer from different forms of addiction, by ourselves, are in the end bait for mental institutions, jails, and mortuaries. Just as soon as any two of us get together to stay clean or abstinent, the power of fellowship enters and makes the difference. Open-mindedness—remaining teachable—is the key to making the fellowship work in our recovery.

54. Accepting Acceptance

Recovery is the process of becoming a whole human being, the center of which is to know that I am worthwhile and to treat myself accordingly. An important part of treating myself as a worthwhile individual is to set boundaries. Usually I thought of boundaries as lines of behavior that others were not allowed to cross without receiving some kind of confrontation. This is an important kind of boundary, vital to recovery and to being a friend, lover, co-worker, and fellow human being on this planet. There is an even more important kind of boundary, however. It is a line of behavior that I do not cross myself because doing so would injure me and my recovery.

Say someone comes down on me all self-righteous and judgmental. As an addict my automatic reactions are to assume I'm in the wrong, to begin justifying myself by becoming very defensive, and then to attack. If I've learned nothing else in my recovery, I've learned that my automatic reactions to most things are dead wrong. Okay, what about my boundaries? I've set a boundary that says no one can treat me like that, and here they are doing it anyway. What good is that?

It's good for a signal, that's what. A boundary is crossed, and I can inform the trespasser that he or she has crossed the line. "It makes me angry when you do that," "It hurts me when you say that," and so on. If nothing changes, and I know I cannot change anyone other than myself, I can change me. The first step in changing me is accepting people, places, and things for where and what they are. It's not a judgmental wallow in self-righteousness. It's nothing more than seeing what is and accepting that it is so. Then, I can change where I am, with whom I associate, and to whom I allow myself to become vulnerable. The one thing I have to accept is my own boundary regarding what I will accept regarding myself.

"You've done this all wrong. You just don't measure up. You're not good enough." The next moment after hearing something like that is important, because in the end, no one but me determines how I feel about me. How I feel about me is a choice.

First I need to check it out. What I heard might not be what was said or meant. As they say, I know that you believe you understand what you think I said, but I am not sure you realize that what you heard is not what I meant.

Anyway, if I heard accurately, then I can either choose to feel rotten about myself and how I am not pleasing someone else, or I can accept that that's where that person is right now. I can feel sorry for the person, even love him or her, perhaps let go of it with a "Thanks for your view." Then I can go on, still whole, still worth recovery, and feeling good about myself. To do that I have to follow the little program poem:

Everyone is where
They're supposed to be.
That means all of you,
And especially me.

—◆—

For today I will work at accepting acceptance. The better I get at it, the fewer bumps there will be on my road to recovery.

55. The Hardest One to Pray For

Self-fulfillment. Loving self-care. Loving myself. How many times have I cried out, "What are these people talking about?" This came to a head when I first heard someone describe an open-ended prayer. It went, "I pray for the best for [so-and-so]." Although simple, it has been proven scientifically that this prayer is effective even on bacteria and seeds, not to mention humans. And it is an easy prayer to say for the benefit of those I care for. It was even an easy prayer to say for those I needed to forgive for past injuries, and praying for them is the way toward the peace of forgiveness. Where I gagged on this prayer is in trying it on myself.

"Dear God, I pray for the best for . . . er, uh—you know. I pray for the best for m-m-ah—" and so on. I could pray up a storm for anyone and anything else other than myself. I used to be able to do any number of "Help me" prayers. They implied I was weak, sick, and probably less than worthy. "I pray for the best for myself," however, was a different matter. When I was the object of this particular prayer, I froze. There was an almost audible voice in the back of my head that said "You're not worth it!" That's my usual signal that there is more recovery work to do.

The program tells me that I am worth it. I'm worth being alive, being loved and respected, and I am worth recovery. I am worth all of the best that the bounty and my effort can bestow upon me. That's what the program says. That very strong little voice in the back of my head, however, had an earlier claim on my soul. It says I am evil, worthless, fit only for pain and suffering. My fellow addicts, however, tell me the voice speaking those words is my disease talking to me. If I get miserable enough, reasons my disease, I'll go back to the numb illusion of escape provided by my addictions. Before acting on that, though, I need to think it through.

Regarding myself as worthless is *not* humility. It is, instead, the route back to the nightmare. True humility is the use of the ability to see reality as it is, and to accept what is. This includes my qualities as well as my faults, my strengths as well as my weaknesses. It also includes my worth: my worth to my friends, to meetings, to the program, to my higher power, and, most important, to myself.

For today I will pray to my higher power for the best for myself, because that's what I want and need, and because I am worth it, even if I can't quite bring myself to believe it right now.

56. Believing What You Know Ain't So

"We're told to go with the flow," said a friend at a meeting, "but every now and then I look down and see that I'm caught in a whirlpool."

Shared another, "Every time I hear 'Go with the flow' I mentally hear a huge toilet flushing."

"Faith and fear can't exist in the same person," offered a visitor.

"I keep remembering," said a fourth, "that Mark Twain called faith 'believing what you know ain't so.'"

— ◆ —

It seems perverse at times to take a society of control freaks and make giving up control their only hope of recovery and serenity, but that is exactly what is required of us. Many of us were reared in brutal homes where the rules changed every minute and when not being in absolute control was virtually a death sentence. And now, what are we told? "Go with the flow. You have a higher power. Trust in the process."

I don't know where the flow is taking me. I'm not always convinced my higher power even exists, or if he does, that he really knows what he's doing. I mean, this is the deity who gave men nipples. And trusting in the process sounds like, "If someone takes a swing at you, lean into it." It seems much simpler and very much safer to stay fully in control.

Still, there are those times when everything seems to be crowding in on me, pressing me down, cutting off my view of hope. Then I know I'm really not in control at all. Perhaps I never was. Maybe my whole life of struggling for control has been little more than illusion—thrashing about at the end of some celestial hook and line, fighting against forces I can't even imagine, getting nowhere except hurt and exhausted.

I am truly in control of one thing: whether or not I recover. I can sabotage myself, make myself miserable, and distort my perception of reality until everything becomes a hopeless trek of endless pain. That is where control takes me now. It seems a comfortable place, however, compared to the risks of letting go. That's when I become infested with "mights." This horrible thing *might* happen or that terrible thing *might* come at me, I *might* fail, I *might* succeed, *I might have to change!*

The grass is not always greener on the other side of the fence when it comes to control. Control freaks feel safest right where they are, even if the grass they are standing on is going up in flames. Yet to recover, to find balance and serenity, to receive all of the gifts my higher power is trying to give me, to become a whole, happy human being, I need to move from where I am. I must change. To do that, control is what I need to lay down.

In the program we hear that faith and fear can't exist in the same person, but those of us who have faith that terrible things will probably happen to us know differently. To recover we need the kind of faith that amounts to trust in a higher power. To achieve that trust, we have to try it out. It's scary, but the only way my HP can show me that he works for my benefit is to try him out. The first step in trying is to release my white-knuckled grasp on control just a little bit. By doing that, the faith I already have will grow and replace the need to control. In other words, to get faith there is nothing I need to do. There is only one thing I need to stop doing: controlling.

Today I'll ride the water, even if it looks like I'm going over Niagara, and see where the river takes me, secure in the knowledge that wherever it is, it's going to be better than where I am.

57. Starving the Inner Chicken

At a meeting an addict was working himself into quite a state, sharing about his fears. There was a test coming up, and he might not pass it. If he didn't pass it, then he wouldn't get a job. If he didn't get the job, then his family would have to go on welfare, and he went from there to the family breaking up and his children dropping out of school and going on drugs and into crime, prison, and suicide. Before he could elevate this chain of projections into another world war, another addict asked, "Nurturing our inner chicken, are we?"

— ◆ —

There are three ways of conducting myself through life that are as natural to me as using. The first is to bull my way through without considering any consequences. The second is to do nothing until I can get someone else's permission, thereby dumping the responsibility for the consequences on another. The third way is to do nothing because doing something scares me. All three ways have their roots in the same thing: operating out of fear.

There are many things I don't do because I am afraid, although I usually tell myself that I don't feel like doing them, I'm tired, and so on. Many times I won't call anyone on the phone for help because I'm frightened that the person on the other end of the line won't want to talk with me, or that he or she might think I am silly or worthless. Often I won't confront people because they might react with anger, or point out to me that I'm not worth any boundaries, or that I am all wrong about everything. Expressing my needs to loved ones is a terror, because my loved ones might not love me anymore. Going to classes, taking tests, asking questions, making mistakes, trying to make a friend, being intimate, standing up for myself, changing, trying something new—all are things that strike fear in my heart. Because of that, I stall and stall and often don't do them at all. As a result of nurturing my inner chicken, I wind up feeling fearful, depressed, hopeless, worthless, and a coward. When I was tired of this way of life and was looking for a better one, a friend told me to make a scare list.

"It's easy," he said. "At the top of a piece of paper write, 'Things I'm Scared to Do.' Then simply list everything you need to do but are frightened to try.

Once your list is complete, go back to the first line, cross out the words 'I'm Scared,' and follow the instructions."

It becomes a 'Things To Do' list. Then, one at a time, I do them. "But if I could do them, they wouldn't be on this list," I protested.

"Oh, you can do them," answered my friend. "It's just that you'll need help. See what help you'll need to do the first thing on your list, go and get it, then do the first thing, and then go onto the next."

It was strange to see that the process of getting help added new things to my scare list. Sharing my fears at meetings, talking things over with my sponsor, using the phone, asking for help, asking my higher power for the courage to change the things I can. But that was when I learned that courage is not doing something without fear. Courage is being dribbling-down-the-legs terrified of something and doing it anyway. With the program, my friends and loved ones, and with my higher power, I can take the risk to challenge a small fear by doing something that scares me. Each fear that I confront grows smaller. At the same time my faith and trust in myself, the program, and my higher power grow.

Each time I give into a fear, it grows fatter. For today I'll nibble a little bit more at my scare list and starve my inner chicken. As I make progress doing the things that frighten me, I also grow in self-worth, trust, and serenity. As I emerge from my cocoon of fear I enter the freedom of recovery.

58. Believing in Belief

"Man, I'm just spiritual road kill," shared someone at a meeting. "I don't get this higher power thing, I don't believe in anything I can't see, and I'm a long, long way from coming to believe." The person asked for feedback and got it.

"You already believe," said an old-timer. "You just don't believe you believe. You're here at this meeting, you shared your doubts and fears with us, and you asked for help. These are all spiritual acts. You're a lot closer to spirituality than you think."

Rachel Naomi Remen once wrote, "There is no situation that is not a spiritual situation, there is no decision that is not a spiritual decision, there is no feeling that is not a spiritual feeling." For those of us trying to emerge from the nightmare with curses against this or that god or religion still on our lips, the spirituality of every act seems silly at first. Is picking your nose a spiritual act? Is eating a pizza or going skiing?

The answer is, of course, yes. Every act, which includes every single aspect of a life, says something about how we regard or honor ourselves, how we regard the people and things around us, and how we see our places in the scheme of things. These are all intangible things, impossible to dissect and put under a microscope. Therefore they are spiritual things. Nevertheless they are matters of the most critical importance to our growth and recovery.

Going to a meeting because I need help is a spiritual act because it honors my goal of recovery. Going to a meeting when I don't need help is a spiritual act because it means I am there for others, honoring their goal of recovery, which also helps me. These are not slabs of beef on a counter or dollars and cents. Without them, however, I will eventually find my way back to the nightmare.

"I don't have a higher power," declared someone at another meeting.

Her sponsor grinned and said, "Everybody has a higher power. A higher power is whatever you reach for when you need help. For a long time my higher power was made up out of drugs, candy, sulking, and fighting. Nowadays I call that my Lower Power. When I was ready to recover, though, my higher power was made from other things. Now it's made from the program, all of the people in the program, the meetings, the phone calls, the laughter, and from this unseen energy that binds all of us into a fellowship of hope and love. And you share at least part of my higher power, otherwise you wouldn't be here."

Today I'll put up with the vague feeling that I'm a hypocrite and act as if I believe until my feelings catch up with reality, which is also a spiritual act.

59. A Trolley Named "If"

If I had just gotten that job—
If it hadn't rained on Tuesday—
If my father hadn't been an alcoholic—
If my mother hadn't been a child abuser—
If I hadn't gotten the disease of addiction—
If children would just listen—
If grown-ups would just listen—
If everyone and everything in the universe
*   had seen things my way, all would be*
*   wonderful.*

We hear the "if" game played in sharing sessions and at meetings, on the street, and on radio and television talk shows. It's one way we try to dump the responsibility for how we are and how we feel onto others, which is one of the dragon's favorite ways to keep us sick. For good reason, the program teaches us that there is no recovery until we run out of people to blame. This also includes ourselves.

If I hadn't been so stupid—
If I had gotten into the program twenty
*   years earlier—*
If I hadn't been so smart—
If I hadn't said what I said—
If I hadn't done what I did—
If I had just been as perfect as I wish I had
*   been, my life would've been wonderful.*

One time at a meeting, after a session of if-pong, an old-timer said, "If my grandma had wheels she'd be a trolley car."

60. "If" Is Just Another Word for "Blame"

For many of us, the "if" game is one way of getting in touch with a lot of feelings that need to be felt before we can begin forgiving and letting go. It is, however, an easy rut to get stuck in. When I was going through one of my initial interviews in rehab, I was asked what my earliest memory was. It was when I was three and a half years old, my mother was in the hospital, and my father, whose occupation didn't make allowances for being saddled with young children, dropped me off at a boarding facility for preschoolers—a kiddie kennel. That night, the kindly old woman who took charge of me was putting my clothes away in a dresser. I remember she looked to me like Mrs. Santa Claus. The room was filled with double bunks full of sleeping children. I was homesick and began crying that I wanted my mother.

"Your mother is dead," she replied.

After this thunderbolt, I peeped up and asked, "What about my daddy?"

"He doesn't want you anymore. That's why you're here."

Now, many decades later, I can see it was this person's way of controlling me, and it worked. I was like a rag doll that night. It was a terrible thing for that woman to do to a child, and the counselor I told it to agreed. "But who is doing it to you now?" the counselor asked.

But, if that woman hadn't lied to me, I wouldn't have had my trust shattered. If she hadn't done that, I wouldn't have had my security and innocence stripped from me. If my father hadn't left me there. If my mother hadn't been in the hospital. If World War II hadn't happened. If, if, if.

The woman who had lied to me was very old back in 1945 when I was left in her care. Thirty-six years later, when I was in rehab, I was still blaming her, and others, for how I felt about myself and the world, and for how my life had turned out. And the dragon knew how to use this to serve my disease. Every time I needed to feel abused and miserable, I would drag out this memory and polish it up. That way I could keep inflicting on myself the pain that Mrs. Santa Claus could no longer administer herself.

In the program we are told that the first step in escaping from a prison is to accept that one is in a prison. What happened, happened. What is, is. What will be depends a whole lot on how much time, effort, energy, and serenity we spend hanging onto "ifs" and "might-have-beens." It's as if the path of recovery is a tunnel that needs to be dug through a hill. The work is slow and hard, but it progresses shovelful by shovelful. Playing the "if" game is taking dirt from outside the tunnel and shoveling it back in.

"If" is the blame word. What happened to me is what happened to me, and no one can fix it, change it, or make it up, no matter how difficult I make it for myself. What was, was. The present and the future, however, don't have to be made out of feeling miserable about the past. Each of us in life is dealt a hand of cards. Our choice, each day, is between complaining about the cards we received or playing the cards we've been dealt to the best of our abilities. For today I choose to leave the deal behind me and to play my hand the best I can. (I might check into a GA meeting, too. There has been entirely too much talk of cards in my writing lately.)

61. Where Is Now?

Everything that happens in life, every thought we think and every action we perform, takes place in the present moment. Many of us have difficulty remembering many of these moments, however, because our minds were elsewhere. Either we were pawing over the past or wading through the future. The usual signs that I am living in the past are anger, sadness, resentment, and self-pity. The usual signs that I am living in the future are fear, worry, and anxiety. In the program the old-timers tell us that with one foot in the past and one foot in the future, we wind up peeing all over the present. More accurately, with one eye on the past and one eye on the future, we become blind to the present.

Now is where life, joy, love, peace, balance, and serenity exist. For many of us, however, it is a hard target to hit. One reason for this is that our non-present-moment wanderings often seem like they are necessary and important things to do. My wanderings in the past, for example, were a real effort on my part to change what was into what might have been, and then to feel gypped, deprived, and miserable because I couldn't change anything. Living in the past I could keep resentment alive, throwing more fuel into the fires of hate and revenge. "I am owed!" I would say to myself, and then once again run through all of the crimes done against me to justify the statement, thereby validating my negative feelings.

Taking my experience from the past as my cue, I would worry about how things might happen in the future. "I failed in the past; I'll probably fail in the future, unless I kill myself with worry first." Then I would write unperformed little dialogue plays in my head, making up things I might say in situations that probably would never happen. "I might screw this up!" I'd think to myself, and then become paralyzed through fear and anxiety, thereby screwing up what I thought I'd screw up. "See?" the dragon would shout at me. "So what's the point in all this recovery stuff anyway?"

Over the years I have learned that the point of recovery is to live life as a human being, and that life takes place *only* between the past and the future. The past is history. The future is theory. Life takes place only in the present moment. *Now.*

So how do we hit this elusive mark, the present moment? The first time I scored and knew it was early one spring when I was in my back yard, muttering to myself about some old resentment. I started to head back to the house when I noticed a gray squirrel standing about five feet from me. For some reason the animal hadn't noticed me, and just sat there with his back toward me. I froze, not wanting to scare it away, and watched. It turned around, saw me, and began examining me, trying to make up its mind whether to run or continue eating. He picked up another sunflower seed and continued eating, all the time watching me. I was hardly breathing or blinking my eyes, every muscle tensed against moving, when it suddenly struck me: I was having a wonderful time! I wasn't mucking about in the past, I wasn't tearing out my hair about the future. I was living in right now, and right there I was perfectly happy.

62. Slippery Places

I see the fresh snow falling outside my window and consider the now. I cherish my present moments, and I've collected quite a few of them over my years of recovery. When I discovered downhill skiing four years ago, my present moments quadrupled. For me, when I'm skiing I can't think about anything other than skiing—not and stay alive. My focus has to be on the present moment; otherwise I'm going to go down on something other than my skis. If I'm on my way down Wildfire and my mind is on what so-and-so said to me last October or worrying about whether some story of mine is going to be rejected, I'm going to find myself off the trail getting a spruce massage.

Even if all I think about is skiing, if I'm thinking about the part of the slope I've already been on, I won't be paying attention to what's beneath my feet, and then I stumble, tumble, and turn the slope into a used sports equipment sale. If I'm looking at the whole mountain, worrying about a tough part that's coming up, I won't be concentrating on the snow that I am on, and I wind up eating a glacier. But if I focus on the present moment and fill my mind with the task at hand, not only do I do my best, I also feel my best.

All aspects of life contain solid program lessons for me. Today I will pay attention to the moment I am in and do my best to learn the lessons that moment has to teach me. In other words, screw writing today. I'm going skiing!

63. How to See the Light

It is the disease that both puts forward the desire to use and disguises it to look like something else—even a desire not to use. Thinking it through, bouncing the reasons off a sponsor, or asking for feedback at a meeting can call the dragon's bluff. Many in the program know that an addict can hit bottom *in* the program, and *without using*.

Hitting bottom is not seeing how much one can use, how much one can lose, how sick one can become, how in debt one can get, how many friends and family members one can destroy, or how much time one can rack up in the local crowbar motel. Hitting bottom is a stage of open-mindedness finally reached when the addict becomes willing to go *to any lengths* to recover.

— ◆ —

"It's best not to be using when you hit bottom," someone said at a meeting. "If your eyes aren't open when the light goes on, you won't see it."

64. Looking for Mr. Fixit

How many times have I seen friends in distress and, picking up my handy program tool belt, leapt into the middle of things with inappropriate suggestions and unwanted advice intended to make everything right once again? Too many times. The evidence suggests that very little gets fixed in this manner. Instead, I usually wind up with one or more persons who are angry with me because I'm sticking my nose in where it doesn't belong. On the other hand, if the objects of my advice actually take it, chances are they will wind up in deeper trouble than before, and be *really* angry with me.

For many years one of my most deeply held beliefs was that there is an answer to my problems out there somewhere and that others do have the power to "fix" me. Since my problems never got solved by others, and didn't go away on their own, I was left believing that others were responsible for my still having problems, which was the foundation for a veritable mountain of resentment. Little by little, however, I have learned that it is no one's responsibility to "fix" me. This is for the simple reason that no one can. Even with support groups, therapists, and the help of a loving higher power, the solutions to my problems must come from within me. Once I accepted that, and began taking action, I started getting solutions to my problems.

None of us likes seeing friends or loved ones in pain, so the desire to get in there and end that pain is very strong. In the program, though, we learn that we sometimes need to go through pain to learn, to open our eyes and our minds as to what needs to be done. That is the quickest way to the end of pain. Mr. Fixit rushing in with a Band-Aid, at best, only slows the process.

—◆—

At one meeting a promising young Mr. Fixit was sharing about how frustrated, angry, and hurt he was because his friends refused his intrusive offers of help and, in effect, told him to mind his own business. A little later in the meeting an old-timer remarked, "My dog once told me that the only person who ever fixed him was not a friend."

Think about it.

For today I'll try to remember that everyone has to walk through their own pain, and that includes thee and me. Our gift to the program and to the miracle of recovery is to be there for each other as the pain is being endured.

65. Know Thyself (Before You Butt In)

How could so many things have gone wrong in such a short time? It was like I was some kind of antimatter King Midas. Whatever I touched turned to shit.

I had two dear friends in the program who had some special children. It was one of the few times I fell in love with an entire family. The existence of this family and my relationship to it became one of my most important anchors to the universe. Then the anchor, the family, began eating itself alive.

It seemed to begin with little things. There were nasty little jabs at each other which seemed to progress to bigger and nastier jabs. To me it looked like depression, anger, feeling persecuted, and taking it out on the children in a thousand subtle and not-so-subtle ways. I thought I saw a wreck about to happen and I didn't know what to do about it. A number of their friends had seen the same things, they were concerned, and they didn't know what to do about it either. Curiously enough, the one person I didn't talk to about this was my counselor.

I became obsessed about this family. My work suffered, my program went down the toilet, and sleep became a nightly ritual combat with my mattress. Then someone with a similar problem shared about writing and sending a letter to his friend expressing his concern. It was, he said, the only way he could know that he had done all he could. So I wrote a letter describing what I thought I saw happening and expressing my concern. I read it to them, they reacted like nitroglycerin hit with a sledgehammer, and the friendship was over.

True, it was a caring thing to do. True, what I thought I saw happening eventually did happen: more pain and conflict followed by divorce and the shattering of the family. Nevertheless, I became the enemy, and I was devastated.

Sometime later I got around to talking about it with my counselor. His interest in my story, though, had nothing to do with the intentions, results, or rights and wrongs of the matter. He was interested in why I had been so obsessed with these people and why I was so devastated now. Then he asked the question: "Do you think it might be that if you saved this family, it might somehow make up for the family you couldn't save? The one you grew up in?"

It was one of those proverbial smacks in the head with a two-by-four. Yes, if I could have saved this family, I believed it would make up for this enormous hole I carry where my own family should have been. My letter didn't destroy this family, and not reading it to them wouldn't have saved them. Perhaps we wouldn't be friends, but maybe we wouldn't be enemies.

Today I keep the focus on myself. If someone else asks for help, I'm there. If I find myself obsessing about someone else's problems, however, I am the one who needs the help.

66. My Eyes Are Dim, I Will Not See

If life seems awful stinky
And you cannot see or hear,
You're down and getting dinky,
And your heart is full of fear,
Don't go and see a shrinkie,
Pull your head out of your rear.
—Anonymous

One of the hallmarks of this disease is what is sometimes called "selective sight" or "voluntary blindness." When friends are being less gentle, they might suggest that you pull your head out of your ass. It all has to do with the frustration of watching another die in the midst of mountains of recovery.

Often it sounds like just so many broken records:

"It was late at night, I couldn't sleep, all these things were running through my head and . . ."
"Did you grab the telephone and call someone?"
"Well, no . . ."

"I got in a fight with my partner, he said such terrible things to me, my heart was broken and . . ."

"Did you grab the telephone and call someone?"

"Well, no . . ."

"I was at this party, I didn't know there'd be alcohol there, a good friend insisted that I take a drink, and . . ."

"Did you grab the telephone and call someone?"

"Uh, no . . ."

— ◆ —

Sometimes I imagine the disciple sitting in a crystal clear pool of water, his tongue hanging out, and with his parched lips he croaks, "Master, I am so thirsty."

"Why do you not then drink, Grasshopper?" asks the master.

"Where will I find water, master?"

The master feels his walking stick and thinks for one fleeting moment about smacking his disciple upside his head, but instead he suggests, "Is not your bottom wet? Could it be that you are sitting in all of the water you will ever need?"

"My wet bottom could be an illusion, master. I must be certain there is water before I can drink."

After a sigh, the master suggests, "Feel with your hands, Grasshopper. Cannot the wetness of your fingers confirm the moistness of your behind?"

"That, too, might be an illusion, master. And even if it is water, how am I to know that it is safe to drink? It might not quench my thirst; it might even poison me."

"Open your *eyes,* Grasshopper, and *look*!"

The disciple opened his eyes, saw that he was sitting in a vast pool of clear water, then he watched as his master knelt and drank deeply from the same pool. When he was finished, the master stood and smiled at his disciple. "What do you have to say to that, Grasshopper?"

"It looks inviting, master, but perhaps your part of the pool is different from mine. When you drink from your end, you appear to thrive. But if I drank from my end, I might be poisoned."

"Grasshopper," began the master, "did you ever wonder why the masters and disciples here at the temple are shaved bald?"

"Yes, master. I have wondered. Why is that?"

"That, Grasshopper, is so that when you stick your head up your ass, *it won't get stuck*!"

— ◆ —

When my disease is doing the looking for me, it is difficult to see any way out of misery, chaos, and destruction. There is the telephone, but a million excuses not to use it. There is my sponsor, but a million reasons not to get in touch. There are others in the program, meetings, program literature, meditation, writing, and asking my higher power for help, and endless excuses why I can't be bothered. "No one wants to be bothered with my problems." "The meetings are too far away." "I know what's in the literature." "Meditation doesn't work for me." "Writing is just a waste of time and paper." "My higher power isn't listening to me anymore."

When I am doing this to myself, it indeed looks as though there is little hope for me. When I see others doing it to themselves, however, I can see recovery all around them. All they have to do is reach. There are voices of recovery out there, and if I am to survive, I need to listen to them, particularly when I know it is my disease holding down the other side of the argument.

67. The Return of the Living Dead

So many feelings, so little understanding of what they are and what to do with them. Before the program, feelings were no problem. We didn't have any. If a feeling, good or bad, began to crowd the horizon, we used. If it was a bad feeling, we'd say, "If you had my problems, you'd use too." If it was a good feeling, we'd say, "Okay, let's party!" The results were the same. We didn't feel and we never learned how to deal with feelings.

Now in recovery when feelings come up, especially when they are unexpected, we tend to react in the same old way: look for something to fix it, eliminate it, hide it, run from it. This doesn't always mean a return to the substances that led us into hell and then recovery. For addicts the ways to try and avoid feelings seem endless. Aside from alcohol and other drugs, compulsive overeating, and compulsive gambling, there are shopping, TV, video games, movies, music, knitting, house cleaning, work, sex, exercise, sports, hobbies, destructive relationships, religion, and the entire range of ego-pumping service and control activities surrounding politics, organized religion, business, health care, community government, school board, Parent-Teachers Association, and Twelve Step Program service work. For the codependently afflicted, there are always others over whom to obsess. "Keep busy and don't feel a thing," is the battle cry.

> *"I've got to get my mind off it."*
> *"I can't dwell in the past."*
> *"How important is it?"*
> *"Don't be a baby."*
> *"Big girls don't cry."*
> *"Real men don't get hurt feelings."*
> *"I must be strong for others."*

However it is said, it all comes down to the same thing: "I'm afraid to feel and I'll be damned if I will." To those of us who have been hurt a lot during our lives, it's easy to understand why we do not want to hurt anymore. The thing many of us find hard to understand, though, is that we will be damned if we don't feel. By stuffing the feelings that hurt, we make it impossible to feel the good feelings. At best, we wind up as unfeeling automatons, spiritual and emotional zombies. On the other end of the spectrum is that constant dull feeling of sadness, depression, hostility, loneliness, and sense of impending doom.

How grateful I was when my first rotten feeling made it all the way through. I was sick and tired of not being able to love or be loved. I wanted to be able to feel again, and my therapist and I worked on it. I was drawing pictures, talking, writing, and not much seemed to work. Then she gave me an assignment which seemed pretty silly at the time. I was to find out where particular emotions were located in my body and determine what colors they were. For example, where is sadness located in my body, and what color is it? In addition, I was supposed to draw a picture of it.

I was stumped for days until I was driving to a meeting one afternoon on a two-lane highway. There was a car in front of me who was going a little too slow, and I pulled out and began to pass. This fellow seemed to have a rather large emotional investment in *not* being passed. He sped up and wouldn't let me get in front. When I slowed, he wouldn't let me fall behind. He was punishing me for daring to try and pass him. A car came from the opposite direction, and I went as fast as I could to get by and only passed the clown by millimeters. Even so, the third car was partly run off the road, recovering only after several hair-raising twists and broadslides down the road.

I was safe, and then it came over me. I was angry. Not irritated, not miffed, not annoyed. I was ripped-ass, roaring *angry*. For whatever reason, this yahoo saw fit to risk his life, my life, and however many other lives were in the third car to serve his particular demons. I was angry, it was spread across my chest, and it was the color of fire: red, orange, and hot yellow. What was even more peculiar was that the anger lasted about two seconds and was immediately replaced by gratitude to this silly bastard who almost killed all of us. He helped make it possible for me to feel.

Today I am grateful for all of my feelings, even pain, fear, disappointment, and all of the others I used to hide from. Today my painful feelings tell me more than that I am hurt. They tell me that I am a human being successfully walking a path of recovery.

68. Watch That Inside Curve

Impending doom. Anxiety. Worry. Fear in all of its subtle and not-so-subtle forms. There are days when, almost before we awaken, we are filled with dread. We search what's going on in our lives to see what it is we are afraid of, but often there's nothing there except the fear. Sometimes it's unfelt fear from times in the past—times when it was dangerous or humiliating to express fear. Sometimes it's something else confused with fear.

"My attitude sucked," shared one addict at a meeting. "I couldn't figure it out, I couldn't let it go, and I couldn't turn it around. I was afraid, cranky, angry, thinking everyone's either against me or doesn't even care if I'm dead or alive. I thought my program was in the toilet and I figured that going back to the nightmare couldn't be far behind. I can't tell you what a relief it was to find out I had the flu. I became instantly better once I knew I was sick."

For those who are trying out their full range of feelings for the first time, there will be many times when we just don't seem to get it right no matter what we do. Unfocused fear, feeling hurt at what someone else thought was nothing, loving and having all of your signals misunderstood, being angry with seemingly the entire world clucking their tongues at your overreaction.

It's like learning how to swing at a ball with a bat. When we're first learning, we miss a whole bunch of times. Even when we've gotten used to hitting the easy ones, a new pitch comes along and we miss again. There is always more to learn. Every now and then, however, a pitch comes, that inside curve you've never been able to hit, and suddenly you slam it out of the park. Somewhere, somehow, you've acquired the skill to meet the new challenge.

It is the same with feelings. There are situations that, again and again, seem beyond us until that magic moment when suddenly everything falls into place. My big terror was confrontations. All I knew how to do was to operate out of fear. When a situation would come up that called for a confrontation, all I knew how to do was ignore it or go berserk. No matter how I tried to justify it, ignoring the confrontation because of fear filled me with shame. On the other hand, tripping off into rage and getting into verbal and physical swinging matches had the same result. I'd be filled with shame.

What I needed to learn seemed to be unlearnable. Yet I listened and shared at meetings, kept going to therapy, and asked my higher power for help. The help came from an unexpected source. Someone who had gotten angry at me called me an asshole behind my back, and I heard it. Usually I would have pretended that I hadn't heard the comment. Before getting into the program, my reaction might have been more violent. This time, however, there was no fear, no overreaction, no hesitation while I tried to figure out what everyone else might think. I was angry. I turned around and did my best Robert De Niro impression: "Are *you* talking to *me*?" He lightened up four shades, began babbling about not getting any sleep the night before, then he apologized, and before the apology was done it was very clear to me that I was not this guy's problem. Anger, response, understanding, letting go, and it was all done. That inside curve was batted up into the stratosphere. Later, at a meeting, strange words came out of my mouth: "Today I was called an asshole, and I'm grateful."

Today I'll try to remember that it is a life of many mysteries, and as long as I remain in recovery, they will get solved.

69. The Aim of the Holy Spirit

"It seems like I've been one step ahead of the dragon for weeks," said someone at a meeting. "I don't go to a meeting unless I'm crawling up the wall. I don't pick up the phone unless I'm cornered by the monsters. They say that this is an action program, but I think I've been working a reaction program, bouncing from crisis to crisis."

Sometimes it's called the recovery turkey shoot, living on the edge, or dancing with dragons. Another word for it is cruising. Whatever it's called, it comes down to the same thing: seeing how little program it will take to keep me in recovery. What's hard for some to understand is that once we have decided to cruise, recovery not only stops, it begins to go into reverse. "In this program," said one old-timer, "there are no plateaus of recovery. Either you grow or you go back."

An action program means making a regular thing out of working recovery: going to meetings, staying in touch with sponsors and program family, working the Steps, perhaps going to therapy or participating in other recovery groups. "The disease is always there," said someone at a meeting. "It has infinite patience and all it wants to do is shoot you down. All we have to remember is to work an action program rather than a reaction program. It's harder to hit a moving target."

Today I'll try to remember what a clergy person in the program once said to me: "Work the program.

You can't be goosed by the Holy Spirit if you're sitting on your ass."

70. One Meeting at a Time

The fellow chairing the meeting seemed a little embarrassed. When it came time for him to share, he said, "On my way over here I had an attack of draggin' bones. I simply didn't want to drag my bones to another damned meeting. I was tired of meetings, tired of working the Steps, tired of the program, and tired of everybody here. Early in my program, though, I heard a story in these halls that has been repeated over the past dozen years at least a thousand times.

"Some poor soul, on hands and knees, manages to crawl back to the program after weeks, months, or years of trying on the nightmare again. Almost without exception, they begin their sharing with, 'Well, I stopped going to meetings.' The exceptions usually began with, 'Well, I started cutting down on my meetings, then I stopped going altogether.' It's such an easy trap. Everyone who shares at a meeting has something to teach me, and I listened to those people with both ears. If I stop going to the meetings, if I stop working the program, the odds are quite excellent that I'll wake up some morning back in the nightmare. I don't want to go back."

Another at the meeting shared, "I'd see those people crawling back through the door, and I'd tell myself that if I did go out again, all I'd have to do would be to get real humble and start over again. That was when I realized how many more of them hadn't made it back to the program. Most of those who go out again stay out and explore hell until they die. I wasn't certain that I had another recovery left in me, so I stayed for another meeting."

"Going to meetings," shared a third, "isn't something I'm going to do for the rest of my life. An endless succession of meetings stretching out for the rest of my life is too much. It's like not using. Going to a meeting is something I decide one day, one meeting, at a time."

The person who was chairing said, "It's like this medicine I take for my heart. As long as I take my medicine, I stay alive. Everything good I have right now I owe to recovery and this program. As long as I take my medicine, the recovery will continue. Meetings are my medicine."

Or as an old-timer said, "If you don't want to wind up as dragon bones, drag those bones to a meeting."

Today I can remember that the program is my medicine. I don't have to like it, be excited by it, or even believe in it. All I have to do is do it secure in the knowledge that the gratitude for having done it will eventually follow.

71. A Really Stupid Suggestion

A woman at a meeting was relating how she had a terrible resentment against someone and it seemed impossible for her to let go of it. What finally worked for her was a "god bag." "Take one grocery bag," she said, "write the name of your higher power on the bag, then write down your resentment on a piece of paper, toss the paper into the bag, and the resentment will go away."

When I heard the suggestion, my open-mindedness developed a terminal cramp. The god-bag idea sounded so stupid that it took me years before I tried it out for myself. Three years later, once again I found myself in my growth mode: in enough pain that I was willing to try anything. In this particular case, I had a resentment against someone who was living rent-free in my head. In the shower this person would be in there covered with suds, buzzing my brain. At night trying to sleep, there he would be happily burning holes in my pillow. Facing yet another sleepless night, I remembered the god bag and decided to give one a try.

I was by myself. No one would have to know about it. If it didn't work, no one would be the wiser. If it *did* work, however, there was another problem I needed to address. I knew myself well enough to know that if I did toss my resentment into the bag and it did go away, I was just sick enough to go back into that bag and retrieve the paper just to find out what it was that had troubled me so much. That was when I came up with the god box.

I took a small cardboard box that had a cover, I closed it, and taped it shut with vast quantities of duct tape. I then cut a slit in the top just big enough in which to insert a folded up piece of paper. I intended the resentment I placed on that paper to take a one-way trip.

Next, on a slip of paper I wrote down the name of the person I resented, what the resentment was all about, and what my feelings were. I folded it up, stuck it in my god box—*and the resentment went away.* I did not know why it worked and I did not care. I was up half the night writing down other things to stick into my god box. I seemed to have a machine that could do for me something I could not do for myself: let go.

Years later, I heard an old-timer in a meeting suggest a god box to a newcomer who was finding it impossible to let go of a resentment. After hearing the suggestion, the newcomer shook her head and said, "Sorry, I don't have that kind of faith."

"You don't need faith," answered the old-timer. "All you need to do is do it."

72. Out of Focus

The bad attitudes were rumbling at the meeting that night. One member of the group had been fired and could see nothing but deprivation, degradation, and hopelessness in his future. The breaks hadn't come to another, and she could see as clear as glass that they never would. A relationship had gone sour for yet a third, and he could not see any way to fix it. The idea of his former friend hating him for all eternity seemed more than he could bear. The entire universe of recovery looked pretty bleak until a tiny voice spoke up from the back of the room. "You know, if all you look for is shit, shit is all you're ever going to find."

—◆—

There are pink clouds, where everything seems wonderful and perfect. There are also stink clouds, where nothing works and everything is one setback after another. Neither pink clouds nor stink clouds give us a balanced, accurate view of reality and ourselves.

"Focus," shared an old-timer, "is what I choose to fill my attention with. If I look only at what isn't working in my life, my life will look as though it doesn't work. If what I choose to look at are only the things that are working, everything will look perfect in my life. It gets worse when I take the things that are working and make them look as though they are failing, or take my disasters and make them look like victories. Both are forms of denial that leave me blind to the real world. For me true humility is accepting the facts of reality, about myself and about the world of people, places, and things outside of myself. To achieve that, I need to see things as they are, not as either I or my disease would like to see them."

Said another person at the meeting, "To get that balanced view I can't rely on the contents of my own head. I need meetings, and contact with others in recovery. It's like with my house. When my dragon is working me, all I can see are the blemishes: work that needs to be done, things that need to be fixed, taxes, bills, the real estate market collapsing, and so on. All I was looking for is crap, so that's all I saw. Sometimes a visitor will see our place and say, 'What a beautiful house you have!' Of course, what I want to respond is, 'Are you crazy? This hole? What in the hell is the matter with you?' I need that outside view to remind me that what I am looking at a lot of the time is not reality. Instead, it's reality filtered through my disease."

His sharing reminded me of my own experience. Years ago my significant other and I moved to a secluded house, our property bordering a beautiful small lake. Plans and desires blossomed into goals, and the goals became mental lists of things to do. Of course, they were also lists of things that weren't yet done. She wanted an enormous flower garden and several extensions on the house. I wanted my own office in a separate building, a natural stone bridge across the stream, a sailboat. I wanted to clear the brush out of about twenty acres of our land, line the paths and roads with rock walls, and blaze a footpath around the lake shore. I also wanted a huge vegetable garden, an amateur observatory, a treehouse, a playhouse, and the list went on. As the months passed, the things that weren't done squatted on us like some huge, smelly, prehistoric toad. Life in our new home took on all of the spiritual charm of a forced labor camp. There was an endless number of things to do, and not enough bodies, time, money, strength, or passion to do them. Soon, all we could see were the things that weren't done and weren't likely to get done. We were living in a hellhole and cursing the madness that had caused us to move there.

One day a program friend dropped by for the first time, stepped out of her car, and said, "Oh, what a beautiful place you have here."

Significant and I looked at each other with concern. Obviously our friend was either saying that to please us or her brain had just fallen out. Couldn't she see what a pit we were living in? The answer, of course, is that no, she couldn't. We were looking at different things. She was looking at what we had. We were looking at what we didn't have.

The safe path for me is to remember where relying only on myself brought me. When things seem darkest, I can share at a meeting, get another point of view, talk to my sponsor, make a phone call to another member, continue working the Steps, read my program literature, or get together with my higher power and make up a gratitude list. If I choose to see nothing but the dark, I am choosing to have my disease do the looking for me.

—◆—

"I'm getting some elective surgery," said a friend. "I'm having the nerve that connects my eyeballs to my anus removed to see if I can improve my shitty outlook."

73. In a Galaxy Far Far Away

It was a familiar story. The recovering person at the meeting had a couple of years in the program and he seemed really caught between reality and a hard place. This wasn't working, that was falling apart, and he didn't know where to turn. What was there left to do but go back to using? That was when a young voice from the back of the room said, "Use the Force, Luke."

The famous line from *Star Wars*, of course, drew a burst of laughter from those at the meeting. The main reason it was funny to those in the program is because it is very true. By whatever name it is called, we need a higher power. Since its first days, it has been a staple of Twelve Step recovery that nothing short of divine intervention could have relieved our suffering. In short, we depend upon miracles. Without miracles we are back on the hell wagon. But what higher power should be used, and what are its rules?

"I just don't get it," I heard someone in rehab complain to one of the floor counselors. "I don't see any higher powers."

The counselor went to a chair, picked it up, and handed it to the seeker. "Here. Try this chair for a power greater than yourself. It can hold you up a damned sight longer than you can hold it up."

In the Steps it is made very clear that the higher power is a god of our own understanding, which means that it doesn't even need to be any of the traditional notions of gods, or even a supernatural being of any sort. We rely upon a power greater than ourselves, and finding and using such a power is a highly individual thing. It is up to each individual to pick the power that will aid in his or her recovery. The magical thing about Twelve Step programs is that *all of the higher powers that are called upon and used work.*

When I came into the program I was engaged in research for a historical novel that required me to gather the facts concerning many ancient religions from the dawn of time to the fourth century CE. Since I was in the process of trying to decide upon a higher power of my own, I decided on a whim to try out all of the religions I was studying. Runes, Celtic animism, *I Ching*; Egyptian, Greek, and Roman pantheons, Mithraism, stone monsters and messiahs, everything from Abderus to Zeuxippe. To my astonishment, *they all worked.* When I consulted the runes for what I needed to know for the day, I got what was most important for me to know. When I prayed to Mithras for the courage I needed to meet a particular challenge, I got the courage I needed. In the reach for higher powers, I've even seen total misunderstandings work.

A woman shared that when she first came into the program in New England, she was very confused. She was willing to try anything, however, and the foggy sense she made out of her first meeting was that she was to turn her will and her life over to the care of this great and powerful Native American deity, Hiahpowah. She asked Hiahpowah for its help for a number of weeks until she became more familiar with the Down East accent, read some program literature, and put two and two together. The point, however, is that Hiahpowah worked just as well as any of the other higher powers used by members in the program. *It is the heart that is important, not pronunciation.*

The force that we each draw upon to aid us in our recovery is there. This is well supported by our continued existence in recovery. The nature of this force appears to be intelligent and capable of helping us achieve, grow, and recover to the degree that we are willing to achieve, grow, and recover. It matters only to each individual in recovery what name this power is called: God, Jesus, The One, Allah, Shiva, the higher or inner self, the Tao, life force, Great Spirit, crystals, the Four Winds, the quantum field, higher power, no name at all, or even The Force. Whatever it is called, it will work, but only if it is used.

Today I will make an effort to increase conscious contact with my higher power, trusting that it will help me in my recovery and all other things, if I let it. Help me, Obi-wan.

74. The Jade Tree

It was one of those times when it seemed as though my higher power had nothing better to do for entertainment than screw up my day. I had just gone through a bad emotional patch, and here I was in another. No sooner had I gotten up than that celestial fist had driven me into the dirt again. I was looking around in my office for something nonessential to smash, when I noticed my jade tree in the window. I had grown it from a tiny branch a friend had given me shortly after I returned home from treatment. Now it was a good fourteen inches high and it was growing a bit lopsided, since the sunlight only came from one direction. I turned the pot around and sat down in my office chair to wallow in self-pity.

While I was there, I looked again at the jade tree. It suddenly occurred to me that my house plant had gone to one hell of a lot of trouble to arrange its branches and leaves to receive as much light as possible from a particular direction. Then I went and turned its pot completely around. It was then that a great secret to acceptance and serenity was revealed to me. In one respect I was the plant's higher power. For the plant's benefit and future development, I had turned its pot. The curious thing, though, was that the plant didn't sit down and whine about this sorry turn of events, or cry, or rage and complain. The jade tree simply began growing in the new direction.

Then it became clear to me. Every now and then my pot gets turned. I can wail, howl, and complain about it, or I can continue growing in what appears to be the new direction. Curiously enough, for neither the jade tree nor myself had the direction changed—only the appearance of direction. The jade tree continued growing toward the sun and I continue growing toward recovery and my higher power.

For today I will listen to everyone and everything that crosses my path, knowing that the wisdom I need can come from anywhere or anything—animal, vegetable, or mineral.

75. Fearing Fear

Anxiety! *Fear!* Oh no, not again!

Often it seems as though I no sooner get through one panic attack than I'm gearing up for the next one. I have a program. I go to meetings. I have a sponsor. I have a higher power. I'm supposed to be immune from fear, aren't I? It's unfair!

Fear is like anger, happiness, and sadness: human emotion. Humans get frightened, and it is fear that protects us from doing any number of self-destructive things. My fear is a message from me to myself. It says, "There's something dangerous. Take appropriate action." Of course, it was my disease's interpretation as to what was appropriate action that destroyed so much of what I was and loved and landed me in Twelve Step wonderland.

Still, with the help of my program, my recovery family, and my higher power, I have a different view of what is appropriate regarding fear. We hear at meetings: "Fear is courage that hasn't said its prayers." Contact with my higher power is always a good beginning as to what to do about anxiety, fear, or panic. Paths of action immediately begin opening for me. What am I afraid of? Why? What can I do about it?

Sometimes I'm afraid because I'm trying to control the future. Will this business investment pay off? Will the audience like me at my next performance? Will my next project be successful? How can I manipulate things to make them come out the way I want them to?

The simple answer is that I cannot control the future. It is out of my hands. The answer then is to let go. Eastern philosophy tells us to do our duty *unattached to outcomes*. Therein lies peace of mind. So, how do I let go of outcomes? I can accept the fact that outcomes are not up to me. All I can do is give whatever it is my best shot and then see what happens. In extreme cases I can write down the issue and stick it in my god box, confident that it will turn out exactly the way it is supposed to. I can talk it out at meetings or with my sponsor or higher power. There are a great many things I can do that are more positive than sitting there wringing my hands or trying to stuff my fear with food, drugs, or some other compulsive behavior.

Sometimes I'm afraid because I'm not doing something, and I'm not doing that thing because I'm afraid. There's a letter I need to answer, but I don't, because the person I want to mail it to might be hurt, disappointed, or angry. There's a challenge I don't meet because I'm afraid I'll fail, or if I succeed I won't know how to handle it. There's a project I'm afraid to propose because some faceless decision maker might reject it, and therefore reject me.

Each confrontation I avoid diminishes me and

makes me smaller to myself. When I become small enough, then I am surrounded by fears. Every waking moment is anxiety-ridden. When I am small enough and frightened enough, I will go back to using.

Each fear I confront, however, proves to myself that I can successfully confront fear and makes me stronger and less afraid. As I confront my fears, I can see my general anxiety level going down.

Sometimes I'm afraid and I just don't know why. It might be something from my past announcing itself as my next issue. It might be something else. It might even be nothing. I recently spent two anxiety-packed days wondering what had happened to my serenity and my program. To explain my fear to myself, I spent a good deal of time looking for things to be afraid of—and finding them. A big performance was coming up, one I had been looking forward to. But now the thought of it terrified me. What if I bomb? Only one person had signed up for a writing seminar I had scheduled and advertised? What if no one else applied?

It got worse. When I cranked up my computer to work out my fear by writing on this book, the entire document was gone! Wiped out! The work of months had somehow evaporated from my computer's memory. Panic is a feeble word to express how I felt. It had been several weeks since I had worked on the book, but how could I have wiped it out? My fear spread to include something I had always suspected: I really don't know how to use my computer.

In another day, hell, everything might be wiped out! I really don't know how to do anything!

With nowhere else to turn, I sent a quick message to my higher power asking what I should do. It took me just a moment to remember that *Yesterday's Tomorrow* was filed away in a different word processing program than the one I usually used. I changed over and there it was. Then I learned that my area had been under a dangerous ozone-level alert for three days. I have a bad allergic reaction to ozone: I get anxious. For the performance, I realized that what I do I do very well. I am prepared, and all I can do is my best. The outcome is not up to me. As for the seminar, I'll send out the advertising, and if there aren't sufficient responses, I'll cancel out. I was afraid because I was afraid. In other words, to strike a familiar note, there was nothing to fear but fear itself.

For today, one by one, I'll do my best to confront my fears, knowing that as each one is confronted, I will become stronger, less afraid, and more capable of confronting the next fear.

76. Miracle Grow

Every now and then at a meeting you hear someone whose problems make everyone else's seem almost insignificant. It's like stewing in resentment all week because you were overcharged on an auto repair bill only to run into someone who was just told he has terminal cancer. After that, somehow the repair bill doesn't seem like such a big deal. I always wondered, though, about the person who wins this dark-side lottery. How does it feel to be the one in group with problems so huge and so horrible that everyone in the group uses you to make themselves feel better about their own problem?

"Gee, against what's happening to you, my troubles don't seem so big."

"I was on the pity pot before I heard you, and now I have something to be grateful for. Thank God I'm not you."

Who wants to be the one carrying such a load of crap that it makes everyone else feel grateful? Let's face it, saying "I'm grateful I'm not you," is just another way of saying, "Buddy, you are in deep caca," which is one step away from saying, "I know how you stay sober. I just can't figure out why." How is the one with the perpetual burden of the week supposed to handle it? Where does that person find gratitude?

In the program I've heard addicts of all stripes refer to themselves as grateful to have the disease. It took me several years in the program, but I now number myself among them. If addiction hadn't driven me into the program and recovery, I wouldn't have the friends I have now, I wouldn't have the positive outlook on the world I have now, I wouldn't have the health, hope, love, and serenity I have now. Hence, I am grateful to be an addict.

Nevertheless, it seems beyond my understanding how a sufferer wasting away with full-blown AIDS could say that he or she is grateful for having contracted the disease, but I have heard it more than once. I have sat dumbfounded as I listened to persons who have lost limbs, their sight, their families, their freedom, and so on, share their gratitude about what has happened to them. I never thought I would be able to understand it until, suddenly, I found myself in the role of group running sore.

When I began facing up to being an incest survivor, gratitude became a dimly recalled memory; a fantasy of my youthful naiveté. After I shared how, when I was four, my mother used to drug me at nights to enable her to use me, and how she almost killed me with a drug overdose because I struggled awake during one of these episodes, suddenly I became everybody's cause for gratitude. I could almost see my meeting mates saying to themselves, "Damn, I'm sure glad I'm not you."

I actually met another incest survivor who told me that she was grateful for her experiences because they helped make her the person she is. She could have been speaking Urdu for all of the sense it made to me at the time. Grateful? For enduring this soul-searing horror? Revenge I could understand. Anger, resentment, pain, sadness, rage, murder, and thermonuclear annihilation I could understand. But gratitude? I figured she must be kidding herself to sidetrack the rage she didn't want to feel, conveniently forgetting that that was what I used to think about those who identified themselves as grateful recovering alcoholics, addicts, and so on.

Three years later, after sticking very close to the

program, doing group work, attending weekend gatherings of male incest survivors, individual counseling, and couples counseling, I was sitting in a very small meeting listening to someone share. The person was a man who had been bouncing in and out of the program for ten years, running from the horrors of active drug addiction on the one hand and the memories and feelings of being an incest survivor on the other. Every time he would get clean, the feelings would explode and out he'd go again to numb himself out with drugs.

Suddenly I found myself being grateful for *all* of the experiences I had endured. Because of them I had been granted two very valuable gifts. The first gift was the growth I had achieved that enabled me to recover. I had become a new person: stronger, more understanding, more compassionate, assertive, loving, trusting—a wealth of things. I owed who I was to all of the experiences I had been through.

The second gift was of enormous value at that very moment. It was being able to share my experience and let that man know that I had been where he was. I could share that recovery is hard and painful work, but that victims of incest can recover. I was on the other side of this raging river he needed to cross. Because of that he knew it could be crossed. I was who I needed to be at that moment, and for that I am grateful.

It was sometime later that I heard the entire matter put into perspective by someone sharing at a meeting. The person said, "Remember: the deeper the shit, the more beautiful the blossom."

77. The Ten-Speed

Step Ten: "We continued to take personal inventory and when we were wrong promptly admitted it."

— ◆ —

I was taking a drive in the autumn countryside, inhaling the crisp Maine air and taking in the colors. While I was filling myself with the beauties of nature, grateful I was in recovery to see them, I was listening to a dreamy classical piece of music on public radio. The music seemed to blend with the day and the mood, making the moment absolutely perfect. All of a sudden the beautiful flute solo was interrupted by dead silence. After three or four seconds of this strained quiet a tinny, distant, but quite distinct voice came through the speaker. It said, "Aw, shit! I did the wrong thing!" The flute solo then resumed.

"That," I said to myself, "was the quickest Step Ten I ever heard."

78. Ups and Downs

Mistake is the "M" word, and criticism is an attack. Never admit to a mistake, not even to myself, and roar fire at anyone who dares to suggest that my way might not be the best of all possible ways. That was how the disease and I jammed me further and further down hell's toilet until the pain became so great that I was finally forced to admit that I had made a mistake. I was wrong. I really did have a problem with addiction.

What a devastating admission it was. I could feel this enormous tower of fantasy and rationalization I had constructed over the years imploding and crumbling to dust before my mind's eye. And if I was wrong about my disease, what else might I be wrong about? The answers have been coming in ever since. Food addiction, compulsive gambling, my being abused sexually when I was a young child, my wife hating me, everybody being against me, my being in control. Most of all, I was wrong about myself, about who I am. I am not some kind of joke my higher power played on the universe, stupid, weak, ugly, and unlovable. I am, instead, a human being in recovery from a deadly disease, and worthy both of the love of others and of my own love.

I heard a speaker at a meeting point out something that had escaped me up until then. She said, "No one is better trained or tries harder for perfection than Olympic ice skaters. Imagine how hard it must be for them to make a mistake. Still, every so often you see them fall on their asses. What then happens is important: they don't sit on the ice and whine, cry, and beat themselves up. *They get right up again and continue their programs.* It's okay to make a mistake. Just don't make a career out of reviewing it."

It became clear to me then how my mind works. If I make a mistake, particularly if I am caught making a mistake, it makes me worthless, stupid, clumsy, and a being utterly without character. What I learned that night was that character is not measured by the number of times you fall on your ass. It's measured by the number of times you get up. Keep getting up.

79. Mess or Message?

It has been said before many times: If the addict wants to recover, you can't say anything wrong. If the addict doesn't want to recover, you can't say anything right. It isn't a program for those who need it; it's a program for those who want it, and so on.

So what do you do when you see someone in the program hell-bent for destruction who doesn't seem to realize where he's going to wind up?

Holding up a mirror to someone in the program is a very caring thing to do. "Here is what I see," and then say what you see. The more traditional way to do this is to begin by saying, "I don't want to take your inventory, but . . ." and then you go ahead and take the guy's inventory. There are several cautions, however.

First, know why you are doing it. There is a world of difference between caring for someone who is hurting himself and pumping up your own ego by becoming a self-appointed group guru. Remember, the sickest person at any meeting is the one who knows best how everyone else's program ought to be run.

Second, are you simply offering information that the listener can either take or leave, or are you on a rescue mission? Trying to rescue and otherwise control someone who doesn't want to be rescued or controlled is the opening pitch in that great national pastime: codependency.

Third, I know I wind up loving and caring about everyone who takes up one of those meeting chairs, if they stick around long enough, and one meeting is usually long enough for me. I don't want to see those I care about hurt, and I certainly don't want to see them kill or die. It is the height of arrogance, however, to imagine that if I care enough and push hard enough that I can save someone.

Here is what I can do: I can tell someone how much I care. I can tell someone what I see them doing to themselves, just as long as I have no expectations concerning outcomes. Few are immediately grateful for that first peek at the mirror. Most important, I can let go and take care of myself. If I am not in recovery when someone asks me for help, I will not be any good to anyone. It is important to carry the message. It is just as important not to attempt to carry the mess.

80. Hollywood May Be Too Late

Speaking of messes, here she was back in another meeting, proclaiming her terminal uniqueness, and other reasons why she had to go out again. One woman who was worried about her said to me, "I know we're not supposed to give advice, and we're not supposed to tell someone else how to run their program, but, dammit, I can't stand watching her hurt herself like this and looking to us for silent permission before she goes and does it."

After that comment, I thought about it and realized that is exactly what our sick sister had been doing. Piece by piece, and bit by bit, she would share her insane plans and her psychotic rationales for them, each time looking around the room, hoping that no one would challenge her. No one would, of course, since letting go and minding our own business are two of the mainstays of getting and keeping ourselves healthy. Some of us, however, are more successful at letting go than others.

Sick Sister was offering as her latest reason for leaving the program the following: "I just don't know where recovery would take me. I'm just going to have to wait until it becomes clear to me."

The woman who had been worried about her got up from her chair, went to the literature table, came back, and dropped the NA Basic Text in Sick Sister's lap. "Here," she said, "Don't wait for the movie. Read the book."

She did, too.

81. Mind over Matters

"No one in the world is as hard on me as I am," shared someone at a meeting. He looked around at the faces in the circle and saw several heads nodding in agreement. "I mean I beat myself up all the time. Back in rehab this was one of the first character defects that was pointed out to me. My counselor asked me, 'If anyone in the world treated you as badly as you treat yourself, what would you do?' That was real easy to answer. I told her I'd kill the sonofabitch." He sighed and looked down at the floor. "But there I was, as big as life and twice as ugly, beating myself up again! How could I be so stupid?"

We laughed and he looked very puzzled at our reaction until it finally dawned on him that in the process of telling us how he beat himself up he was beating himself up all over again.

Someone did mention later that addiction is not a disease of stupid people. It's just a disease. Another addict added that beating yourself up never was part of the program. "One way I found to stop beating myself up," said a third, "is to grant myself at least the same respect that I would give a complete stranger."

When we first come into the program we are a long, long way from treating ourselves like human beings. Step by step, though, each day we move closer to health and recovery. It has been said, "It gets better. It doesn't always feel better, but it always gets better."

82. Crime and Punishment

A long time ago, as a small child, I began punishing myself. I lived in a home where both parents were addicted, as well as an older brother and other brothers and sisters who were affected by the disease in several of its less pleasant forms. Survival for me seemed to depend on pleasing unpleasable people. It seemed that my life depended on me never making a mistake. In a system where the rules changed minute by minute, however, I couldn't help but make mistakes. In such cases I instinctively knew that my best defense was immediate, convincing, devastating remorse. Before anyone else could lay a hand on me, I was in there punching the crap out of myself.

It makes me cringe to think of the things I used to do to show a sufficient quantity of remorse. There was, of course, crushing guilt, endless depression, and a constant repetition of all of the charges that had ever been made against me. I was so evil. It was because of me my father was an alcoholic. It was because of me my mother was a drug addict. It was my fault that the house was always a wreck, my fault my parents could never go on a vacation, and so on. I'd deface and wreck things that I loved, beat my fists bloody punching the ground, set fires and burn myself, and several times cut myself with razor blades. All of this said to those who threatened me, "See? I know I was wrong and I'm taking care of it. You don't have to hurt me. I'll make certain the little bastard never makes another mistake."

As strange and sick as it sounds, this was how I survived childhood. Not so curiously, beating myself up became normal for me. I'm comfortable being uncomfortable. Besides, I didn't know any other way.

That's why, decades later, I was still doing the same things: destroying things I loved to punish myself, punching walls and getting my hands X-rayed, not allowing myself any kind of fun, and scooping up endless oceans of perpetual depression, which was a great reason to continue using drugs. My addiction locked in my self-condemning behavior.

In the program, with alcohol and other drugs behind me, I discovered that the behavior hadn't changed. Being good to myself, which I was told to do, was something I had to learn. The first step was accepting that what I was doing was doing me no good, that I needed a new way to live. That new way involved some big changes.

I stopped calling myself derogatory names, I stopped blaming myself for all of the troubles of the world, I stopped taking the blame for things that weren't my responsibility, I stopped putting myself down with jokes, and I gave up trying to please everyone. I began telling myself that I'm okay, I began congratulating myself when I did something well, and I began trying to please myself. And, although I almost broke my jaw doing it, when someone gave me a compliment I began saying "Thank you," instead of "You're crazy." I haven't perfected it yet, but that's okay. I don't have to be perfect today. As Roman physician Aulus Cornelius Celsus wrote almost two thousand years ago, "There is no legal obligation to perform impossibilities."

83. The Town Drunk

Sometimes at meetings and during one-on-ones I tell the stories of other people who can no longer tell the stories themselves. It's my way of keeping them and their good works alive. At one meeting in the middle of winter, I was reminiscing with someone who had come into the program when I did. We were remembering an old fellow in the program who had been dead for a few years. We shared some memories, and suddenly I had an urge to go out to the cemetery where about fifty program people and I had been for the ceremony when the old guy was buried.

After the meeting I drove out to the cemetery. It was located far from town on a lonely stretch of road. There was about six inches of snow and ice on the ground and there were no cleared paths. As I searched through the headstones, many of which were level with the ground and concealed by the snow, I thought of the town drunk. That was how he used to begin his story when he shared at a meeting. "I was the town drunk."

He was tall, toothless, stooped over a bit, clad in rough clothes, and walked with the aid of a heavy steel leg brace. He drove a huge boat of a car and was responsible for taking hundreds to their first Twelve Step meetings. He would talk about how the doorknob on the front door of the liquor store used to talk to him, and about this burning coal in his stomach that would burst into a roaring fire when he put alcohol on it.

When I came into the program he seemed nine days older than God and was four years sober, which seemed like forever at the time. He had severe emphysema, which was rough in the days when our area had nothing but smoking meetings. It finally got to the point where he would sit in the chair nearest to the door trying to get some air to breathe. It was torture, yet there he would be at his meetings as regular as the sunrise, that smile on his face and that incredibly kind look in his eyes.

One time he needed an operation and at the hospital got hooked on the drugs with which they treated him. When he was released, he showed up at our NA meeting and shared about the drug problem, what he was doing to stay clean, and why he "belongs in this club, too." By then state law had made all public meeting places smoke-free, which helped. Nevertheless, his emphysema progressed.

One day I was working in my office when someone in the program phoned to tell me that the old guy was dead. He wasn't sure of all the details, but the person who called him told him that he had finally died of his respiratory disease.

It was so sudden and unexpected. Everything came to a crashing halt as I both missed him and cursed myself a thousand times for never telling the old guy what he meant to me. What would it have cost to tell the guy that I loved him and that his words and his kindness had done a lot for me and my recovery? How big a risk would I have had to take to give the guy a damned hug? And now he was gone. If I could just tell him what he had meant to me.

That's when the phone rang and the person who had given me the bad news had a minor correction to relate: "You know I told you he was dead?"

"Yeah?"

"Well, I might be wrong about that. He just walked by my window."

That night at the meeting, the old guy was slightly stunned as I and several others leaped on him at once, hugged the stuffing out of him, and burdened him with tearful expressions of love and gratitude.

As the months passed the emphysema continued to grow worse until every breath caused intolerable pain. Sometimes he wouldn't stay for the whole meeting, and then he started missing meetings. One night I saw him at a meeting. When he shared he took up a considerable piece of time, telling his complete story from beginning to end, leaving nothing out. I heard from others that the next night at another meeting, he did the same thing. This was unusual for him. Although he always shared, he usually only spoke for a minute or so. At the meeting the next night, the old guy showed up again. When he shared, he did the same thing he had done at those other meetings. He told his story about being the town drunk, about the doorknob and the burning coal. When he was finished he stayed to the end of the meeting and talked and visited awhile.

He wasn't a materially wealthy man. What he was doing with these unusual sharing sessions was leaving all of us the only thing he had: his story. He left us his experience, strength, and hope. That night he took a gun and ended the torture of his emphysema. Much of the recovery community was at his funeral out at the cemetery, and enough tears to wash Hell clean. At the funeral I imagined coming out to the cemetery every now and then to say hello, but things came up, time passed, and I just didn't get around to it.

After attending that meeting, as I dug one headstone after another out of the snow, I again felt like that time when I'd gotten the phone call telling me that the old guy was dead. If I had only. If I had only come out to the cemetery on a regular basis, I'd know where the damned headstone was. Before I managed to get into really punching the crap out of myself, I saw another row of ground-level headstones and decided to clear just one more. I scraped the snow and ice off it, and there was his name. I cleared the area around the stone and found a number of bouquets of dried and artificial flowers left by others. I wasn't the only one who remembered him. It's still a "we" program. I told him again that I loved him, grateful to have been able to tell him that when he was alive.

84. Recovery Spoken Here

There they are: the program slogans. "One day at a time," "Think," "First things first," "There but for the grace of God," "Easy does it," "Live and let live,"

"Let go and let God," "Keep an attitude of gratitude," "Take what you need and leave the rest," and so on. They are repeated so often in and out of meetings that they frequently seem to me to have achieved the status of ritual prayer. A problem is expressed, the high priest of recovery mutters a few sloganish incantations over the sufferer, and by magic the difficulty should be eliminated.

As with most rituals, however, the application of the slogans often has us nodding without understanding. "Let go and let God," we are told, and we nod at the words, hoping that their magic will somehow find an application to our problems. When the problems don't go away, we find ourselves bewildered and suspicious. It is at such moments when some of our more cynical brothers and sisters will mutter things like "Keep an attitude of platitude."

For me it often takes the rewording of a slogan for its wisdom to get through. For example, at one meeting I dragged in one of my disease's favorite problems: righteous anger. There are all kinds of imaginary angers that my disease cooks up: taking things personally, looking to be a victim, and the eternal "Why me?" The imaginary angers usually dissipate with the light provided by sharing them at meetings.

Righteous anger, however, the genuine, authentic, appropriate, let-God-be-my-witness, this-sonofabitch-done-me-wrong type of anger, seems permanent. This is the kind of anger that is the result of a really crappy thing someone has done to me. I can line up a jury of angels, clerics, judges, program old-timers, and blabbermouths on truth serum and they would be unanimous in saying: "That was a really crappy thing that guy did to you." *That* is righteous anger. What to do with it, however, is another matter.

Somehow "Let go and let God" doesn't seem up to the task. I'm usually left with fifty different ugly head trips as my fantasies try to manipulate apologies and reparations out of the wrongdoers or otherwise make what happened not have happened. The program finds a way, however.

I had dragged my righteous anger into a meeting, talked about it, and was buffing up my row of seemingly infinite resentments when the person who was chairing the meeting said simply, "One of the biggest accomplishments I ever made in recovery was to let assholes be assholes."

A light went on in my head. True, I had been wronged. True, the wrongdoers were assholes. And even more true, I was consumed with trying to change them. Let assholes be assholes. It took a week for me to realize that the official program way to say the same thing is: Live and let live.

Today I can live and let live because I now know at least a part of what that slogan really means.

85. Apathy

Apathy. I just can't get worked up over this topic. There is that joke, though:

"What's the bigger problem: ignorance or apathy?"

"I don't know and I don't care."

86. Breaking Up Is Hard to Do

A program mate in a hurt once said, "Relationships would be a whole lot easier if you just didn't have to deal with people." Another friend said, "Ever since I got into the program it's been telling me to let down my barriers, and every time I let my barriers down, I get overrun by barbarians."

There once was what I thought was a very safe place. I found it as a child, and it did protect me. My safe place was to allow no one to get close enough to love. Every time I trusted someone, I was betrayed; every time I allowed myself to be vulnerable, I was wounded; every time I loved anything or anybody, my heart was broken. This is the lot of a child growing up in an insane, diseased home. Long after leaving that home, however, I still hid behind those barriers.

Everyone I knew could leave me, turn against me, betray me, and I wasn't going to get hurt. Like some kind of emotional feudal baron I stayed locked up in my castle, standing guard, and keeping a watchful eye on all those out there who might possibly be enemies. I was safe and protected against everything except loneliness.

In my program of recovery, however, little by little I ventured out from behind the walls. Many of these early forays were disasters. I had too little training, almost no experience, very little in the way of spiritual and emotional equipment; and I suspect that in many cases I became a saboteur working for the other side.

In time, however, I learned how to love and how to be loved. The walls are mostly down, and every now and then the barbarians rush in and trash the place. A person who was one of the dearest friends I have ever had heard a lie, believed it, and tossed away years of valuable friendship. No matter what I tried, there was no way to budge the lie. There was nothing to say, nothing to do. It was ended.

First came denial. "This can't be what I think it is. This can't be as bad as I think it is. This is just some kind of grotesque misunderstanding that I'm sure I can clear up."

Then came pain. Buckets and buckets of pain. It's finished and there is nothing left but loss and desolation. "It's over. It's over."

Soon after the full pain comes a scramble to put some distance between myself and the pain:

> *"Well, I guess there never was a real friendship in the first place."*
> *"What's wrong with me? How can I change to fix this?"*

"After all we've been to each other!"
"Maybe I'll go back behind those walls."
And so on.

I began writing letters and scripts for conversations in my head explaining, defending, justifying, accusing, blaming, and praying that either through reason or manipulation I could repair the break.

Nothing worked and the pain remained.

"Everybody is where they are supposed to be, Live and let live, Let go and let God, Trust the process, Look for the lessons."

Still the pain won't go.

Finally I get to acceptance. "That's the way it is." I don't like pain, and the most pain in a relationship that is ending comes from fighting the change, refusing to accept the new state of affairs. Once I have accepted the change, it will still hurt.

"But what am I supposed to do with the pain?" demanded someone at a meeting.

The answer came from the back of the hall. "Say 'Ouch!'"

Pain, like anger, love, sadness, and happiness, is part of being a whole human being. Feel it and understand that it is not forever. Know, as well, that feeling the pain is what makes it possible to feel the love.

87. What's Your Sign?

Is there a spiritual higher power? Are there signs to follow? Messages that I can understand and use? Is there an actual light that shows the next step? Is all this spirituality stuff in the program a bunch of claptrap some persons use to kid themselves into recovery?

Questions. Doubts. Shards of a faith shattered. How hard it is to trust once that trust has been crushed beneath the weight of a diseased misunderstanding.

Proof is what I needed to believe in a higher power, and what I would consider proof was very limited. There were living miracles all around me in the form of my fellow recovering addicts, but this wasn't proof enough. I needed something special, something that would show me that this higher power thing believed in me as much as I was supposed to believe in it.

One of the first things I did was test my HP. Riding around searching for parking places has always been one of my major frustrations. "Okay," I said to my brand new HP, "find me parking places." The parking places I have gotten ever since are so good they are embarrassing. Considering the scope of a human's life experience, this might seem a rather trivial matter to place before one's god, but the issue wasn't parking places. The issue was: does this HP exist, does it care about me, and will it deliver? I can't say that all of those beautiful parking places convinced me one hundred percent. It did, however, keep my mind open. More evidence came later.

I was in Boston at a convention and I was having a really crappy time. I wasn't being treated right, things were going all wrong, and I was stretched between rage, depression, and revenge. Serenity was a mist lost in a thunderstorm. After the convention, I was on the Mass Turnpike going west to get the hell out of there and go home. I was so worked up, I decided to test my higher power once more. "What's going on? What am I doing wrong?" I demanded. "Show me a damned sign!" Just then, to my left, painted in gigantic letters on the side of a business building, I read the following:

BARRY CONTROLS

"Now that," I said, "is what I call a sign!"

It has been asked before: Can you read the writing on the wall? I can, but only when I look.

88. Pooch-Anon

Addiction is a family disease. I first heard this in treatment. No matter who uses the substance or behavior, everyone gets sick. A compulsive gambler's life eventually revolves around the bet, and the lives of the gambler's family eventually revolve around the gambler. Addicts, overeaters, alcoholics, it makes no difference. Although the second saying inscribed above the doorway to Hell is "I'm only hurting my-self" (the first is: "I don't have a problem"), the fact is that every using addict affects those around him or her, at home, with friends, with co-workers. How far this aspect of the disease of addiction went astonished me when I returned home from treatment and found that my two cats cringed and ran away every time I raised my voice.

It's strange how this bothered me. I felt sad and guilty about the persons I had affected. But I was *mortified* at how my pets regarded me. The degree of my disease's influence on my cats became even more obvious when a third cat was added to the household. I would scream "Get off the bed!" and the first two cats would vanish without even touching the floor. The new cat would glance at me with an expression that said "A little less noise, please," and then continue licking her paw.

In time, as recovery reduced the screaming and increased my affection, all three cats became healthy enough to ignore me until it pleased them to acknowledge my existence. And then a dog came into our lives.

We bought a house, the owner had an inconvenient dog that he was going to kill (his euphemism was "send to never-never land"), and my wife and I decided to take the dog along with the property. About ten minutes after closing we realized we had just acquired a pet who belonged in Pooch-Anon.

The dog despised all women, was terrified of all men, snapped at little children, and every time anyone raised his or her voice for any reason—anger, joy, laughter, just to be heard—the dog would begin shaking violently and would insert itself between speaker and audience, and would frantically stroke its head against the person's legs as if to say, "Can't we all just get along?" It was a perfect replica of the caretaker role I myself had filled as a child. My mother would either be full of drugs or short on drugs, roaring around the house like a battle goddess looking for fresh enemies to slay, and I'd stand in her path and try to fix whatever it was.

My dog sometimes goes to meetings with me, and I can't help but believe it's helped her. She now loves everyone and has a lot of fun. If voices are raised she still leaps in to make things better, but the leaping takes longer and her shaking now is pretty much limited to when she is about to get a bath. With time, love, sanity, and recovery, all of us are getting better.

89. The Recovery Olympics

I was attending a friend's recovery anniversary, and the group putting on this particular celebration had rented a gymnasium and put on a banquet. Those celebrating anniversaries were called up, presented their medallions, and then told their stories. My friend's story was pretty hairy, involving everything from prisons to psychiatric hospitals, and he was celebrating seventeen years of sobriety. As he was returning to his table, he paused several times to shake hands with well-wishers. One of these folks said, "Congratulations, and remember: you owe it all to your higher power."

The man with the seventeen years raised his eyebrows and slowly shook his head. "No I don't," he answered. "When my higher power was doing it all by himself, you should have seen the mess."

—◆—

Recovery is a team effort. At the barest minimum, it is the addict working together with his or her higher power, the program, a sponsor, and with those in the program. In addition to this can be added rehabs, therapists, counselors, places of worship, and so on. "The main danger in making a higher power one-hundred-percent responsible for my recovery," said an old-timer, "is that it makes it real easy to climb back into addiction and blame it on my higher power."

Today I am a member of team recovery, and we are going for the gold.

90. The Credentials Committee

When my home group was young it was small, which is one reason why the few men in the group who had some time wound up sponsoring females as well as males. In a few instances this resulted in problems, but one young woman I sponsored dealt with and presented unique problems altogether. She was a lesbian and our top relapse queen. After a lifetime of abuse, this woman trusted no one. The only reason she extended enough trust to ask me to be her sponsor was because of a temper tantrum I threw. The tantrum happened like this:

In my aftercare group there was a young woman who was a talented musician and performer, as well as an incredible wit. In an aftercare session one night, she opened up to us and revealed that she was gay. She shared about the hardships this had caused in recovery, how she had to edit her sharing stories to keep this part of her life secret, and how it was tearing her in two. It was wonderful finally getting to meet the real her, and we told her that in the midst of a dozen hugs. That was, however, the last time I ever saw her.

My guess is that she had second thoughts about being open with us. In any event, she went back out and we learned some weeks later that she had died of a drug overdose. It was right after I learned of her death that I drove to the relapse queen's apartment and roasted her up one side and down the other. In between the red-faced bellowing and fist shaking, the essence of my tirade was that I had just lost from my life a really neat person who was afraid to share herself and work the program and that I didn't want to lose another. That's when she asked me to be her sponsor. One of the proudest and most grateful moments in my life was when I got to hand her that one-year medallion.

A few months after that, my anniversary came up and she wanted to chair the meeting. The event she put on in my honor touched me very deeply. It was a large meeting, and by the time it was over I felt so warm and fuzzy I thought nothing could bring me down.

After the meeting I was heading for the coffeepot when someone pulled me aside. "You know," he said, "you shouldn't have had her chair this meeting."

Since she had done a wonderful job, I asked, "Why?"

"She's one of *those*," he answered.

My head was racing. Here before me was the face of that intolerance, the fear which greased my after-care mate's skids back to hell. But, I reminded myself, everyone is where they're supposed to be. Live and let live. Who am I to judge? I took a deep breath and asked, "One of those, what?"

"You know. She likes girls."

"So do I."

His eyebrows curled into a frown as he got right to the heart of the matter. "She is a lesbian and she should not be chairing a meeting."

My answer to this self-appointed chairman of the credentials committee was, "You know, the only qualification for membership in this club is a desire to stop drinking. You don't have to be an asshole, too."

Okay.

So I might have been a bit judgmental. So be it. Intolerance kills. That is why I refuse . . . er . . . to . . . uh, tolerate it.

Hmmm.

All right, there are better ways I could have handled that. I could have shared my experiences with intolerance in the program and how it has ruined recoveries and has killed some of those I love. I suppose I owe this guy an amend, and as soon as I become willing to make it, I'll do it.

91. Reframing Reframing

It was a beautiful winter day and the snow was falling, adding a few more inches to the mountains where a friend and I would be skiing in a couple of days. As I was looking forward to that, I heard on the local news that a man had just pleaded guilty to killing someone for turning around in his driveway. Immediately I flashed on the insanity of my using days. I knew exactly where that poor bastard was coming from, because I had come quite close to being there myself. I remembered the resentment-fed rage against those I felt were taking advantage of me, a rage that, each moment, moved me closer and closer to the point where I wouldn't take it anymore.

Years later, in recovery, I met a little old grandmother at a support group meeting in the same condition. She had a grandson on drugs, and a very startling way of sharing. She pulled a .357 Magnum hogleg revolver from her purse to show us what she carried at night as she drove the streets of our friendly little town looking for drug dealers to waste.

We urged her to leave her gun at home, since, among other things, the chances were good that she'd wind up smoking her own grandson.

By the grace of a patient universe, I never acted on any of the times murder filled my heart. When I was still using, I would fuel myself with vengeance fantasies until carrying a loaded gun to take care of trespassers, rude bureaucrats, inept professionals, and passing motorists seemed sensible. Thankfully I entered recovery before acting on this twisted view of things. I gave the man who killed the fellow in his driveway a "There but for the grace of God," prayed again for the pistol-packing grandmother, and continued with my day.

Later, while I was clearing the snow from the rather long driveway to my house with a snow thrower, I caught sight of someone behind me. It was a cross-country skier cutting across my property. By the time I could get my tractor turned around, the fellow was gone, and so was my serenity. My property was posted and there was no way that the bastard didn't see the signs. He just didn't give a damn.

Old vengeance fantasies began teasing my head, and then I remembered the man I had heard about on the news. Thanks to recovery I had a clear choice between sanity and insanity. I chose sanity, but the anger would not go away. That was when I remembered the "reframing" technique mentioned in the book *Emotional Intelligence*, by Daniel Goldman.

Reframing means "consciously reinterpreting a situation in a more positive light." For example, instead of "He saw the posted signs and just didn't give a damn," I could choose to tell myself, "He probably didn't see the signs" or "Perhaps he was lost, or maybe he had an emergency." These were real possibilities, not just attempts at kidding myself out of my anger. Yet I was reluctant to reframe how I saw things. That was when I learned that there was a price on this reframing business: a willingness to forgive and to let go of routes back to the nightmare.

The program teaches me that forgiveness isn't something we do for someone else; it's something we do for ourselves. We are taught as well that resentment isn't something we do to someone else; it's something we do to ourselves. I don't want to go back to the nightmare. That's why I became willing to forgive, which allowed me to reinterpret what happened, let go of the situation, and be sane.

According to the Federal Bureau of Investigation's *Uniform Crime Report* [for 1989–95], there are in the United States alone over twenty-two thousand murders a year. That's more than nine for every hundred thousand persons. If addiction and obsessive/compulsive disorders in all their many forms were removed from the equation, I wonder how many of those twenty-two thousand murders would ever happen. But they do happen, and none of those homicide victims will have addiction, or compulsive gambling, or codependency listed as a contributing cause of death.

Choose sanity, and before the mouth runs or the lead flies, make a nice day. Lives depend on it.

92. Stiff Joints and the Scientific Method

"What difference should it make to a real higher power what position I'm in when I pray? Standing, kneeling, flat on my back, or sitting on my butt, a prayer is a prayer."

The person at the meeting who had just finished sharing about how he prayed on his knees looked at the speaker and said, "You're one of those Horizontal Baptists, eh?"

As I listened, I knew that I was certainly one of those Horizontal Baptists. When I, at last, gave in and began using a higher power, I considered the matter of prayer and kneeling. I am a rational man, a believer in science and common sense. It's a higher power of my understanding, right? I'm the one who designed it and picked it, right? Besides, what difference does it make to a god, for crying out loud, whether I'm kneeling or lying down when I pray? That makes sense, doesn't it? So, why in the hell does the prayer thing work a hundred times better when I do it on my knees?

One person at a meeting suggested that the "Send" buttons on the intercelestial transmitter are located on one's kneecaps. "I meditate sitting down," responded another. "Does that mean that the 'Receive' buttons are located on my ass?"

I don't know. I think it has something to do with not wanting to pray on my knees. I know I don't like it, and one of my big fears is being caught on my knees praying. Perhaps refusing to pray kneeling is my way of holding back on humility. A prayer pretty much means that I can't do it by myself and that I need help. If there is this part of me that is holding back, I am saying I need help, but not really. In other words, I don't really know what I'm praying for. Is it any wonder, then, why so few of these prayers manage to connect?

Let me put it like this: In the process of being relieved of my various addictions, I did alcohol and other drugs sitting on my butt using the group and the program for a higher power; I did compulsive gambling lying flat on my back praying to St. George; and I did my obsessive depression with being an incest survivor back on my butt communing with the universe.

Compulsive overeating, for some reason, does not budge unless I get on my knees. When I get on my knees and ask for a day free from that first compulsive bite, I get it. When I try praying in any other position, it just doesn't work.

What about rationality? What about common sense? What about science? Well, the scientific method, rationality, and common sense all tell me to do it the way that works. Praying on my knees works, so that's the way I do it.

Come to think about it, out of all of the praying positions I've described, kneeling is the only position which I am not accustomed to using for eating. Hmmm.

93. The Damned Program Doesn't Work, Opus 912

The person sharing was sounding pretty desperate. "When I was writing down the resentment part of my Fourth Step, listing all of those I resented, why I resented them, and what my part in it was, I realized that most of the times I had injured myself. As I realized that, one by one the resentments went away. I was free of them and there was no one in the world who believed in the miracles of this program more than me. Then, after a few weeks, one by one the resentments started coming back. Pretty soon I was back in the whole damned stew again. The program's not any better than those self-help books that make you feel good for little while then dry up."

"You may be right," said a visitor from the opposite side of the room, "but I'm wondering if there isn't something you forgot to do."

"Like what?"

"Like Step Five, Step Six, Step Seven, Step Eight, Step Nine, Step Ten, Step Eleven, and Step Twelve." The hot blush from the resentment man was a pretty good answer to that question.

There are many miracles in the program. It is a process of miracles that stops when the addict stops working the program. Momentum will carry the addict along for a while, then comes the inevitable fall. The disease is progressive and relentless. A recovery program that is half done will probably work fifty percent of the time.

Or to put it another way: A newcomer demanded to know, "Why do I need all this stuff—higher powers, sponsors, meetings, all these damned steps, the telephone, and all this reading and writing. Why do I need all of this?"

The fellow who eventually became the kid's sponsor asked, "You ever try to build a car with just a screwdriver?"

94. The Old-Timer

So there I was: four months out of rehab in Waterville, Maine, my wife and I celebrating the miracle of our fifteenth wedding anniversary. The miracle, of course, was that there *was* a fifteenth wedding anniversary after the dual meat grinders of addiction and codependency. We chose Waterville for this revelry because our regular weekly aftercare session took place there at the local rehab. We went to a movie and ate dinner at Pizza Hut; then, about two hours before the session began, I freaked.

All of the withdrawal I went through in rehab hit me at the same time. I tried to stop the feelings with predictable results: a five-alarm anxiety attack that literally had me climbing the walls. Shakes, sweats, headache and joint pain—it reminded me of some of the mornings I thought I had left behind for good. Flashbacks are very useful in that regard. They are previews of coming attractions should I decide to go out again.

It just seemed to be getting worse and worse, and I didn't know what to do. If I had had a sponsor, I could have called him, but I didn't have a sponsor. If I had had some phone numbers, I could have called someone, but I didn't have any numbers. If there had been a meeting, I could have gone to that, but we didn't know of any meetings at that hour. In several hours, however, there would be a meeting at the rehab where we did aftercare, and sometimes the recovering folk show up early. My wife aimed the car at the rehab, and we flew.

When we reached the floor for addiction recovery, I grabbed the first grizzled-looking old-timer I could find, sat him down, and unloaded. I dumped how I felt, not just the pain and panic, but the embarrassment. For some reason, going through that flashback in front of my wife was the worst kind of humiliation. I must have talked for an hour, and when I was done, the panic attack was over. I was feeling much better and very grateful to this wise recovery elder who had loaned me his ears, so I asked him, "How long have you been in the program?"

He looked at me with sad eyes and a wan smile as he said, "All day."

95. All the Right Credentials

When I first came into the program, I was very picky about who was qualified to help me. First, it had to be someone my age or older. I was thirty-nine, and the sole meeting I went to in those days was one at a college with almost nothing but college students. Slim pickings, and if I had bothered to share my qualification list to anyone else, they probably would have pointed out to me that the dragon was the one who wrote it. Other qualifications for someone who could help me: he had to be a man, of course, as well as being a writer, musician, or artist. Curiously enough, there was no one in my group qualified to help me.

They did tell me to take some phone numbers, and that was easy enough to do. After all, I never used the telephone, so what threat could they be? I had about fifteen numbers, and I ranked them from top to bottom according to the likelihood of the person being able to help me, considering the few qualifications any of them had. Then came decision time.

I was in my office writing something when I got a call from the bank. The details of the problem are lost to time, but the result is still fresh in my mind. I was betrayed, I was hurt, I was angry, I was frightened, because the dragon was sitting on my desk and saying, "Okay, here's the deal: Call someone for help or go out and drink. There are no other choices."

I really panicked then, because no one was qualified to help me. I looked at my list of phone numbers and decided to at least try. I dialed my top number, a salesman who was male and was, at least, older than I was. No answer. The next one was a teacher. He was at least my age. No answer. And so on down the list.

I dialed and dialed and no one was in. By the way, there is a special seat in Hell waiting for those benighted miscreants who put cute messages on their answering machines.

Finally I was down to my very last number and was in a serious panic. I didn't want to go back to the nightmare, and I was at the end of my rope. I dialed the last number, that of a nineteen-year-old college girl with seven more days in the program than I had. She was in, she came right over to my house, we talked, and the panic was over. That was when I learned that the only qualification a recovering addict needs to help me is to be a recovering addict. To carry our particular burden we are endowed with a special kind of magic: the ability to understand and help each other. That's why the program, the meetings, sponsorship, and the phone work.

96. Spiritual Grease

I agreed to go to rehab, finally, after I decided I could work up a pretty good poker game there. A woman I met in rehab got there because she was pregnant and her doctor told her that drinking would be bad for her future heir. She couldn't stop, and the rest was history. Another fellow was there because his lawyer said admitting his problem and going through rehab would look good at his trial. An international drug dealer was there, essentially, hiding out from the law.

One man, from the moment I first met him, did nothing but complain about the place and complain about the evaluation that said he was an alcoholic. He said he was not an alcoholic and that those people simply didn't know what in the hell they were talking about. This confused me, because I knew he had admitted himself to rehab voluntarily. I asked him why he had agreed to go to rehab. He frowned at me, shrugged, and said sheepishly, "I didn't think I'd have to do it sober."

There was a woman in my group who woke up one morning to see her entire family, employer, friends, and an intervention counselor gathered around her bed. "Before coffee or anything, they pulled their god-damned intervention right there and then because that was the only time they could catch me sober."

My favorite was a man whose daughter had gone away to a drug treatment center. Some weeks later, he and his wife showed up at the rehab for their daughter's family week. Once he had gotten through the front doors, his wife yelled at him, "Admit yourself, go through the program, or don't come home!" Then she jumped back into the taxi and slammed the door. As the cab was pulling away from the curb, she shouted out of the window, "By the way, Julie doesn't have a drug problem!"

Weirdly missed turns that got someone into their first meeting are also common. About ten minutes after one meeting in a church basement had begun, a woman wandered in, took a seat, and began listening to the speaker. About five minutes later she stood up and began edging her way toward the exit. A moment after that she returned to her seat and stayed for the remainder of the meeting. Around the coffeepot afterward she shared that she thought she was attending the church's finance committee meeting, and by the time she discovered this was not the finance committee, she had heard enough to skip the finance committee meeting.

At conventions related to my writing, my wife and I usually hold sort of an ecumenical Twelve Step meeting, all comers welcome. We post copies of the following sign on bulletin boards, in the elevators, and here and there:

FRIENDS OF BILL W.
AA, Al-Anon, OA, NA, GA, SLAA,
Or whatever A saves your A
One Day at a Time,
Let's Get Together
Meeting Date:
Time:
Location:

We always manage to attract a few, and meetings during conventions are often lifesavers. The very first time we did this, there were about ten of us at the meeting in our hotel room when this fellow, about two-fifths over a gallon, came reeling into the room. "Where the hell is Bill? I'm a friend of his!"

He looked around the room, frowned, and asked, "What is this?"

One of our number told him, and his face grew a shade redder with each elevation of his eyebrows. "Well," he said at last, "I guess I'm in the wrong place."

"You think so?" asked a man near the door. "They tell me that everyone is exactly where they're supposed to be." The wanderer didn't stay, but perhaps a seed was planted. And maybe it was fertilized by the literature one of us sneaked into his pocket on his way out the door.

Once at a meeting a well-dressed man dropped in and wanted to know from us whether we thought he was an addict or just having a bad week. He related his tale of woe, and we listened. "No one can decide that for you," answered the guy sitting next to him, "but, speaking for myself, I don't believe anyone makes it in here by accident."

Today I'm not so picky about how I made it through the doors. I'm just grateful I did.

97. The Better Way

A visiting relapse king dropped by our meeting one time and used his sharing time outlining, in convoluted detail, why he was going to stop going to meetings. He suspected his anonymity had been broken, and his evidence was something he thought he overheard about something someone else might have said maybe about some-one that might have been him. There was also someone at his regular meeting who had a strange look, and some people at another meeting who weren't working their programs.

The recovering addicts in our bunch had learned long ago not to give our silent permission to commit suicide. When he was finished, therefore, one of our number leaned toward him and said, "You're wearing yourself out, man. Easy does it. If you're trying to talk your way out of recovery, any argument will do."

— ◆ —

When I first came into the program, I had the outlook of a hemophiliac in a briar patch. I was afraid that the program wouldn't work for me and I'd be forced back into the nightmare. I also was afraid that the program *would* work and I'd never drink or drug again. And let's face it, the program was asking some pretty ridiculous things of me: attending meetings full of strangers—drug addicts and alkies—I mean, who knows where they've been? Talking to them about myself and my feelings—I mean, is this demented, or what? A sponsor? A higher power? *Trusting* my higher power, a sponsor, the program, and the process? These people were *insane*!

Every now and then, though, some poor bastard would crawl in and talk about how he had cut down on meetings, went out again, and proceeded to lose whatever he hadn't lost before. Almost every time, the arguments such persons had used to talk themselves out of the program were, coincidentally, some of the same arguments I was considering. Therefore

173

I made a rule for myself that probably saved my life. I would continue going to meetings until I found a better way. When I found that better way, I would go to my next scheduled meeting and let the other junkies in on the good news. I mean, why keep such a miracle to myself? So far I've found a dozen or more "better ways." However, I have yet to find one that doesn't look and sound really stupid to me by the time that next meeting begins.

98. *Ist Das Nicht Ein Guruschmuck?*

Tradition Two: "For our group purpose there is but one ultimate authority—a loving God as He may express Himself in our group conscience. Our leaders are but trusted servants, they do not govern."

—◆—

I once heard a program officer defined as someone who goes around giving advice to people who are happier than he is. It has also been said that the sickest person at any meeting is the one who knows best how you should run *your* program.

I don't suppose anyone should be surprised at the existence of these poor souls. Take competitive, perfectionistic, control freaks, have them arrive at the conclusion that they are addicted and must work the program to recover, and chances are you are going to get a fair percentage of folks doing their best to become perfect alcoholics and addicts. Not surprisingly, program officers often find their way into service work where they can "run things."

Yes, Tradition Two says we have no leaders, but a true program officer can put a spin on the term "trusted servant" that would have any of several twentieth-century despots nodding in admiration. Just as many of us used to "need" drugs to try and keep a lid on things, the true program officer "needs" to be number one to feel whole. Filling your mind with other people's problems helps avoid the rather unpleasant task of looking at your own problems. Being in charge and having others do what you say is a big ego stroke which says, "If these guys are looking to me for help, maybe I'm okay after all."

Everybody is where they are supposed to be, and I've put in my own time marching in lockstep from meeting to meeting. The problem is, program officers and their advice cause damage and cost lives. They look and sound authoritative, and some newcomers, eager to do the right thing, gobble up these controlling pearls of wisdom, and follow them straight out of recovery.

I have seen program officers boycotting certain meetings (that have caught on to what they are doing) and work other meetings badmouthing the one they no longer attend. There is one such person I know who forbids his sponsees to associate with certain other members of the program or to go to certain meetings. Since all of this bad blood is picked up by those who simply want a loving, accepting environment in which to recover, those who would have come into the program may go elsewhere and look for something else.

I don't know what the answer is. There is a very thin line between being enthusiastic about the program and being obsessive. I have yet to see a program officer who, when confronted about his or her behavior, did anything other than get defensive, quote the program literature like scripture, and act like a wolverine with hemorrhoids sitting on a cactus. I gave up my own badge and made a few amends only when I saw the damage another program officer was doing.

I suppose the best defense is to realize that some are sicker than others and that this is not a reason for looking elsewhere; it is a reason for staying in the program and adding the sickest of us to our prayers. Today I need to remember that giving up on my own recovery because of someone else's behavior means the disease, not me, is in full control. I remember, as well, this little poem:

> *Behold the program officer,*
> *He hasn't got a clue*
> *How to even recover*
> *Anyone but you.*

99. The Pooch Within

"Today," began a woman before the meeting, "I am definitely in touch with my inner baby."

"I know what you mean," said a young man. "At the supermarket today the bagger said, 'Have a nice day.' I told her, 'Sorry. I've made other plans.'"

"Hell," joined in a third, "When I was at the supermarket to buy some bananas, I asked for Panama yellow!"

"Into each life some rain must fall," said Longfellow. I quoted that line to the campus cop who was opening our meeting room one time and who was, in the process, filling the air with the burdens he had undergone during the day. He was *really* in touch with his inner baby. As I quoted the line from Longfellow, intending to comfort him by suggesting that he was not the only one the universe had singled out for a bad day, he took it that I was accusing him of engaging in self-pity. Explanations and assurances to the contrary notwithstanding, he was determined to have a bad day and to blame me for a share of it.

The man who was with me said, "It was like watching a dog chewing on its own tail and barking from the pain."

"I guess there wouldn't be much point in telling that to the dog, would there? He already knows he's biting his own tail."

Inside at the meeting the topic was bad hair days, and there were two telling comments. The first was the joke about how most people, when they get a flat tire, call a mechanic. The addict calls the crisis hotline. The other came from a wise old fellow who pointed out that all of us can start our day over at any time. All we need to do is decide to do it.

Today is going to be a pretty good day—sooner or later.

100. Green Beans and Ham

I was experiencing my own peculiar form of writer's block, which takes the form of a paralyzing lassitude. Some days it is all I can do to drag my butt up the stairs, turn on the computer, say "To hell with it," and try and find something else to do. Interestingly enough, this is the book that had me jammed. The proposal for it had been out since Christ was corporeal, nothing seemed to be happening, and I was beginning to think along the lines of taking what I had, printing out a few copies for family and friends, and getting on with a serial-killer novel I had been planning.

Even at this stage of recovery, I cannot say that I rely totally upon myself for my feelings. If an editor is enthusiastic about a story I'm doing, the completed pages fly like a blizzard. I can do a novel in five weeks with sufficient pats on the head. When all I get is dead silence, though, I tend to fill the void with negatives.

So there I was, with the choice between staring at my monitor or cooking up the ham and green beans.

I went for the ham and green beans. Therein lies a tale of woe.

We need to begin with the garden. First, because of business, I was late with the planting. Then, to make up for last summer's drought, it rained and rained and rained. When my wife and I went away on another business trip, the couple who were house-sitting for us were enjoying a thunderstorm, watching it through a window, when they saw a bolt of lightning hit square in the center of my garden. What it comes down to is there wasn't much of a harvest.

There were enough green beans, however, for our traditional batch of ham and green beans. Which brings us to the day when I dumped writing on *Yesterday's Tomorrow* to make ham and cursed green beans.

The pot I selected was almost a family heirloom. In went the ham, the cleaned green beans, and water. I put it on to boil. While I was waiting for it to boil, an idea for a meditation popped into my head, which goes to show that the cure for almost any creative blockage is to simply let go. I ran upstairs and began typing a few notes, which led to completing the meditation, and beginning another.

About then there was an annoying noise coming from downstairs. We had recently installed a new electronic doorbell, and I reluctantly tore myself away from my writing and went to an upstairs window. There was no one pushing the doorbell, so what was—

"Oh, hell! The smoke alarm!"

In a flash I remembered leaving the pot with the fire on high and I didn't even know how long ago that had been. The stench downstairs was remarkable, although there weren't the huge black clouds I had projected. There was a bit of a haze, and I turned off the burner. One look beneath the pot lid brought forth the black clouds.

The dinner was ruined, the pot was history, and the house smelled like a depressed skunk had swallowed a hand grenade. My wife was at her antique store. As I phoned her, I remembered to try to be positive.

"Yes?" she answered.

"Hi, honey. Guess what?"

"What?"

"The new smoke alarm works."

101. An Occasional Exception

We are not supposed to give advice at meetings. There are several reasons for this, not the least of which is the doubtful quality of the advice. Few of us are well enough, experienced enough, or know another well enough to advise someone else upon his or her life problems. Still, there are times when all of the powers of the universe point to an exception.

There was a Twelve Step member who had been wandering in and out of the program for fourteen years and had spent the three years at that meeting showing up drunk. His longest period of sobriety during his fourteen years coincided with his longest stay in jail.

Sitting next to him at the meeting was a very shy old-timer who hardly ever shared. For him, saying anything about himself was a burden. Handing out unsolicited advice was unthinkable. However, the drunken member was again talking about how he had been stumbling around in the program for a long time, ever since the first time the court had ordered him to attend Twelve Step meetings, but his life just didn't seem to be getting any better.

The old-timer, his voice shaking from nervousness, said, "You know, the program works a whole lot better if you stop drinking."

Curiously enough, that comment turned on a lightbulb, beginning the unhappy member's sobriety, which thus far has lasted more than twenty years.

102. Planning Ahead

The theme of the rehab lecture was total abstinence from all mood-altering drugs. The inmates' discussion continued into the patients' lounge where, later, there would be a Twelve Step meeting. One of the inmates was quite distraught. "Do you mean I won't even be able to have a drink of champagne at my own daughter's wedding? It would insult her and her husband's family!"

"Use ginger ale," suggested a group mate.

"Or that nonalcoholic sparkling cider," suggested another. "It even comes in a champagne bottle."

The protester was not soothed. "Apple cider has nothing to do with marriage. When I stand before my daughter's wedding company and raise my glass to toast her future, I can't do it with dishwater. Even if no one else knows, I will."

There was a fellow leaning against the wall. He was one of the members waiting to attend the Step meeting afterward. He asked the father of the bride, "How old is your daughter?"

The inmate frowned, blushed, and said, "Four." We all laughed.

"Always supposing your daughter ever gets married, and you're still sober and alive, why don't you decide this one on the day of the wedding? By then maybe you'll have some pretty good reasons of your own for sticking with the cider."

— ◆ —

What about communion? What's God going to think if I use grape juice?

What about mouthwash? Am I supposed to stink?

What about cough medicines? Am I supposed to just cough?

What about business luncheons? Am I supposed to close a big deal with a Kiddie Cocktail?

What about friends? If I can't keep up with them, what'll they think of me?

What about diplomatic dinners? Would the premier of Russia be impressed with a toast of seltzer and lime?

It's been said before: if you want out of recovery, any argument will do. There are nonalcoholic mouthwashes and cough medicines. It takes a little time reading labels, but recovery is worth a little extra time. With business lunches, most men and women in business prefer clear heads. If you don't want to drink, you'll have lots of company. If a fellow at the luncheon insists that you drink, that's *his* problem. You might invite him to come along with you to a meeting. Chances are he'll never urge you to drink again. Friends that insist you drink for their friendship to continue have made your death the price of their friendship. You can make a better deal. And the next time you get appointed secretary of state, you'll notice that quite a number of your fellow diplomats are teetotalers because of religious prohibitions. And, speaking of religions, if your higher power insists on you consuming alcohol, smoking pot, or doing peyote or other drugs to be righteous, it's time to get yourself another higher power.

If you want to recover.

103. True Love

Conventions are program intensive-care units. Regardless of the program, it is a chance to meet hordes of others in recovery, spend three days attending meetings and workshops, and generally saturate yourself in recovery. At my third attendance of one I go to in Maine, I had almost four years in the program and was staring in wonder at the force of denial.

It was the morning of the second day, and there were about twenty of us in a workshop on relationships. There was a young guy talking about his loneliness and how he was thinking about dumping his girlfriend and looking elsewhere. He loved her, he said, but things just weren't working out.

He began describing his girlfriend and some of the things she had done, and I don't think there was any doubt about what was going on. This guy had a girl who was busting a gut loving him, and he couldn't allow himself to be loved. He couldn't accept it, take it in, and feel good about it.

As they say, if you don't love yourself, no one else can convince you they do. As I was about to lay my insight on this poor soul, something rang a bell. I felt exactly the same way that this kid felt. Then I remembered this thing I used to do when I was so young I was barely able to walk. I would cry for love. "Nobody loves me," I would cry, and what I got in return was laughter, ridicule, and an occasional beating.

When I was older, about seven or eight, I no longer went around saying "Nobody loves me." However, I still felt the same. I felt that I did not matter to a single person on Earth. I remember telling my mother that I was going to hang myself. She said, "That's nice, dear." So I went and got a rope.

I went out to a concrete bench that was next to a willow tree. My father and older sister were outside working on something, and my father asked me what I was doing. I told him I was going to hang myself. More laughter. My sister said I didn't have the guts. I made a noose, tied it to a branch, placed the noose over my head, and jumped.

It was a very clumsy attempt at manipulation, but it worked. By my actions I forced my father and sister to act to save my life. On some strange level, I mattered. From my mother, though, I got a three-hour-long lecture about how offended she was that I did not know that she loved me, not to mention how I had risked damaging the willow tree. The theme ran along the general lines of "I love you, goddamn it, and if you ever try a stunt like that again, I'll beat you within an inch of your life." It went on for so long that by the time she was finished, I was damned near ready to go out and hang myself all over again.

So there I was, half-resigned to living a life without love, listening to another guy who was making it very clear that this lack of love was something we both were doing to ourselves. I could see any number of things that were lovable about the guy who was sharing. He just couldn't see them. That's when I turned the focus on myself.

Was there anything about me that was worth loving? Almost four years clean and sober, a year away from gambling and two years from compulsive overeating. I had a good sense of humor, cared about others, and backed up that care with action. There was the courage and perseverance to face a number of monster issues. I was working the Steps, making amends, doing service work. I wrote novels and stories that a lot of folks thought were important to them, I did beautiful wood carvings, and—

I was stunned at the possibility that I just might be lovable. Then I remembered how, just before our fifteenth anniversary, my wife had stolen my wedding ring from my junk box (for a long time I was too fat to wear it, and when I could wear it, I didn't care). She had taken it to a jeweler and had something engraved in it. I vaguely remembered passing it off as nothing and forgetting it. Suddenly I had a compelling need to see what was engraved inside my ring. As the meeting went on around me, I took off my ring and did some of the most important reading of my life:

R TO B 5-4-67   LOVE 5-4-82

—◆—

Love?

Love?!!!

Me?

Could it be possible?

I stood up right in the middle of the guy's sharing and said, "I just discovered I'm lovable. You are too. Bye." I hugged the stuffing out of him and ran out of the room. I went to my room, grabbed my bag, and was racing toward the main door when the chairman of the convention hollered, "Hey, Barry! Are you running out on us?"

I hollered back at him as I ran for my car. "I just discovered someone loves me, and she's ninety miles thataway!" I gestured toward the north, hopped in my car, and didn't get a speeding ticket the whole way back home. The cop car hasn't yet been made that can catch true love.

104. The Secret

A young recovering addict and I were before a sixth-grade class whose teacher had invited us to talk to her students about addiction and recovery. My companion was fifteen, and he told the war story while I shared mine, emphasizing the family end of the disease. I talked about how hard it had been for my sisters and me in school, coming from an addictive home. They were overachievers, hoping that approval in the form of grades could make up for the lack of approval elsewhere. My route was underachieving. I couldn't concentrate, I never tried anything I wasn't absolutely required to do, and my outlook on the future was "What's the point?"

The home we grew up in was abusive in just about every meaning of the term. Depression and fear were constant companions, and every minute was taken up with survival.

I talked about how it makes no difference who drinks or drugs, the whole family gets sick. The family can recover, however, and I talked about support groups like Nar-Anon, Al-Anon, and Alateen. I never got to take advantage of Alateen; I was almost forty when recovery had some meaning for me. I talked, however, about being an Al-Anon member and an Alateen sponsor, and what those programs can do for suffering family members.

After our talk was over and the class was heading out to recess, the teacher said that one of the students wanted to talk to us in private. Soon the room was empty of students, except for a twelve-year-old girl. She came up to us, and she looked haggard. Her eyes squinted, she had age lines around her mouth and dark circles beneath her eyes. She stood there, her shoulders hunched as though she was trying to be invisible, the knuckles on her fists white. It made me tense just to look at her.

She wanted to know about Alateen. Her father was an alcoholic, her mother was into prescription drugs, and she didn't know what to do. We told her about the two Alateen meetings in the area, and she was quite a distance from both. It would have to be a secret from her parents, and they had to know everything about anyone who came to see her. She wasn't allowed out of the house in the evenings— during meeting times—and if her parents ever found out she was attending something like Alateen, they'd kill her. What should she do?

I looked at the boy and he looked at me. What should she do? I was damned if I knew. All I could say was something I had heard in rehab: The most important thing is to admit that you need the help. Once you've done that, the how will present itself.

To be honest, it sounded lame as hell right then. I went home, stared at a wall, and felt depressed enough to call my sponsor and talk it out. Then the young boy who had accompanied me called me up to talk out the same thing. He was depressed as hell.

Somehow, we made it through the night, and the next day, and the next. For unrelated reasons, it was necessary to stop going to the Alateen meeting I had been attending, and I managed to force that girl's unhappy face out of my mind. The world is full of suffering, and all I can do is all I can do. Still, every now and then, the look in her eyes would come back to me, and my mind would fill with what I considered the program's—and my—failure.

A year later the same teacher had me out to her class to talk to her current crop of students about writing. I love doing this, because I am always full of ideas and enthusiasm when I complete one of these gigs. After the talk was over and the students were rushing out, the teacher asked me if I'd stay behind. There was a seventh-grader who wanted to say something to me.

The teacher went to the door, opened it, and nodded. A beautiful, self-confident girl came in, her face radiant. I didn't know her, but she got up on tiptoe and whispered in my ear: "I'm in Alateen."

I stared at her, and bit by bit I recognized that wizened, hunched up, wired-down bundle of nerves that had asked me about Alateen the year before. She was, literally, a new person. I'd never had anyone who wanted to share such a secret with me, and I confess, as we exchanged hugs, I started blubbering. Afterward, as I flew home in my car, I said to myself, "I'll be damned. Once you've admitted you need help, the how *will* present itself!"

105. The Sound of One Hand Clapping

"What is the sound of one hand clapping?" asked the Zen master.

The student put down his joint, meditated a moment, exhaled, and asked, "Left hand or right hand?"

"It doesn't make any difference," responded the master.

"Sure it does," insisted the student. "The left hand goes 'cl, cl.' The right hand goes 'ap, ap.'"

—◆—

Two years into the program, the above joke was all I knew about the subject of meditation. In rehab I attended a meditation workshop, but halfway through the relaxation exercise, I relaxed, fell asleep, and only woke up when everyone else was leaving the room. Three years before I went into rehab, shortly after my heart attack, my doctor suggested meditation as a way to manage stress. He sent me to someone who had the local spiritual franchise. Candles, Hindu gods, chanting mantras, all with the promise that if I got it right I could hop around on the floor like a frog. Chanting my mantra didn't seem to do anything for me unless I had a few beers and a couple of Ativan first. I grew discouraged and quit—the meditation, not the beer and pills.

Years later, in the program and looking at the prayer and meditation parts of Step Eleven, I once again became interested in meditation. I went about it like a true addict: ask no one and do my own research. By the time I was finished looking over Buddhist, Christian, Confucian, Hindu, and Islamic meditative practices, I was thoroughly confused about what meditation was, what good it was going to do to my recovery, and how to do it.

In my nontheistic way (God forbid I should actually pray), during a meeting I sort of wished for some kind of enlightenment on the purpose of meditation. Later in the meeting someone shared: "Spirituality is like a radio set. Prayer is sending; meditation is receiving."

It is amazing how, after months of studying turgid tomes of the world's wisdom on the subject of meditation, some recovering drunk in a meeting makes a joke about a radio and it all becomes clear to me. That's why we go to meetings and why those wishes we call prayers (and those prayers we call wishes) are important.

106. Tuning In

Meditation is not just sitting there being bored or listening to the echoes in my brain rattle around. Meditation is clearing the channels for incoming messages—what one Internet surfer I know calls receiving his G-mail. Is the higher power who is sending these messages a Judeo-Christian god, a mountain, the Great Spirit, the inner self, the other self, Jung's great friend the "unconscious," or the quantum field? It doesn't matter. Whatever it is, however each of us regards it, the messages will come through, if we meditate.

How to meditate? Some Buddhists practice mental concentration by meditating on a particular topic. They list forty different subjects of meditation, among them colors, lights, recollections, and virtues. Do I listen to noise, sit in the dark, tie up my leg like a pretzel, chant gibberish, or what? What will be right for me?

Again I was at a meeting and again I offered my wish for enlightenment on how to do this meditation business. Someone was sharing about when she first got into the program. Her sponsor had told her, "Sit down, shut up, and listen."

Suddenly a light went on in my head. This is how to tune in my spiritual radio. As long as my head is buzzing with all of this crap about how, who, what, where, when, and why, meditation will be impossible. However if I sit down (get comfortable, relax), shut up (shut down the mental buzz parade, stop thinking, stop analyzing), and listen (be open and aware), then the messages can come through, if they exist at all. I decided to try it.

Meditation, I found, is like any other skill. The first efforts can be disappointing. The more you do it, though, the better you get at it. During one of my early efforts, odd snatches of memory kept wandering into my awareness, and I eventually became skilled at gently chasing them away, keeping the channel open. There was a period, then, where I was completely relaxed, my mind was completely open, and I awaited the message. Suddenly I felt like I had been punched in my lower back. The sensation was so unexpected I let out a yelp. Days later my doctor explained that I had been very tense due to extreme stress that dated back, most likely, to my childhood. In my case, stress centers in my back. What had happened was that a muscle group suddenly let go of its fear and relaxed for the first time in decades.

In subsequent meditations I've gone on head trips through strange worlds and dimensions, received feelings that met needs of mine, received insights to problems, and received blessed peace of mind. Everyone has to put together his or her own best way of doing meditation. I like to put on a recording I have that resembles chanting in an echo chamber. It is not intrusive and it has no beat. It also blocks out noises that might distract me. Sometimes I use incense. It's a way of setting aside a special environment for my meditation. I sit in a chair, close my eyes, do some deep breathing, relax, and listen. I do it for about fifteen minutes, although more than once I've been taken on trips that have lasted more than an hour. The point of it all? Closer contact with the power that makes it possible for me to enter and remain in recovery.

107. The Higher Power Players

My higher power speaks to me through everyone and everything around me. An evening breeze, a joke, my sponsor, someone on TV, something written in a book—all kinds of things. Every now and then HP will put on a theatrical performance. The first one of these productions that I remember was in rehab.

I was getting ready to walk out. I had a billion good reasons why I didn't belong in rehab and only a couple for why I ought to stay: I had a problem with mood-altering drugs, and I didn't know what to do about it. They were pretty small reasons next to all of the crap I was going through. All of the time I was wasting and all of the time they wanted me to waste after I got out, going to meetings, talking to sponsors, doing Twelve Step work, and so on. There was all of this crying, bad feelings, mood swings, and the rest of it. Hell, who needed it? I was a barrel of impacted gloom, and getting out of the rehab program seemed to be the solution. That's when I went to the floor kitchen to get a cup of coffee and the curtain went up on the Higher Power Players.

There were two other patients in the kitchen, a boy of around seventeen and an old guy that looked to be in his seventies. They were talking to each other, and as I made my coffee, I couldn't help but listen.

"I'm just getting started in life," said the boy. "It's not like I've been partying for twenty years. I haven't had any fun yet. What am I doing here?"

"What about me?" asked the old guy. "I'm almost seventy years old. My life's almost over. What's the point in trying to change everything now?"

It was pretty clear that this pair was busy talking themselves out of recovery. They were both silent for a moment, lost in their respective wallows, when I said, "I'm right in the middle, so I guess this program is meant for me."

Exit, stage left.

Curtain.

108. Making Priorities a Priority

If there is ever a Recovery Hall of Anonymous Fame, carved in stone above the main doors will be: "Before Everything Else, Recovery." If we've heard it once we've heard it a thousand times, "If you want to recover you must make your recovery more important than anything else." This is what is meant when the newcomer is asked, "Are you willing to go to *any* lengths to recover?"

An old-timer made the point by asking a newcomer if she'd be willing to give up her children to recover.

The newcomer's eyes went wide in horror as she looked at this crazy old woman to see if she was joking. From the expression on the old-timer's face, her question was no joke. The newcomer thought hard about the nightmare, about the mother she had been—about the monster she had been—without re-covery. Eventually she agreed. If she had to give up her children to recover, she'd do it. The old-timer gave her the good news that she wouldn't have to give up her children, but that she would have to keep up that level of commitment.

—◆—

It was at an NA meeting where I heard it put another way. There was a fellow at the meeting who was sing-ing a familiar tune. "There are enormous demands on my time between my family, the night classes I'm taking, and my business. I'm just getting back on my feet financially and I have to scrabble just to keep my head above water. I just can't take the time to go to all these meetings, much less spend all this time writing, making Twelve Step commitments, and all this other stuff."

A not-so-old old-timer said, "If you make any-thing more important than your recovery, you will lose your recovery. What's more, you will also lose whatever it was that you made more important than your recovery."

—◆—

I need to keep my priorities clear, because when-ever they get hazy I might lose my way and find my-self back in the nightmare. Without recovery, I lose everything else.

109. Not Really Our Kind

The first time I heard it was in rehab at a lecture. The counselor giving the lecture was describing the recovery program, and when he was finished he opened the floor for questions. The first question was this: "You said that the program here for addicts is complete abstinence from all mood-altering drugs, right?"

"That's right," agreed the lecturer.

"Well, what about alcoholics?" asked the inmate.

There were any number of snide comments the counselor could have made. Instead he said, "An alcoholic is an addict addicted to the drug ethanol."

"Well, if alcoholics are addicts, then everyone who drinks, including the president of the United States, is a drug user. That means that bartenders, brewers, and grocery stores are drug dealers."

The counselor smiled and said, "Now you've got it." The smile disappeared and the lecturer said, "People, a drug is a drug is a drug. With the disease of addiction, remember that being a snob is the kind of denial that can get you killed."

— ◆ —

At one NA meeting we had a visitor who couldn't find an AA meeting. After a while he said, "If I understand it right, you people seem to believe that alcohol is just another drug. Isn't alcohol really something different from drugs?"

"The difference between drugs and alcohol?" responded an old-timer. "It's like changing seats on the *Titanic.*"

— ◆ —

If you are going to recover, eventually you have to accept that alcohol is just another mood-altering drug. Still, the question will be asked: "Isn't there at least a difference between an alcoholic and a drug addict?"

"Yes," I heard an NA answer at a meeting. "An alcoholic will steal your wallet. A drug addict will steal your wallet, too, but he'll help you look for it."

110. Working the Serenity Prayer

The only argument available with an east wind is to put on your overcoat.

—James Russell Lowell

"The program is a lifelong study on how to apply the Serenity Prayer." Someone made that comment years ago in a meeting where the topic was acceptance. I remembered it again a few days ago when I returned to Maine from attending a close family member's funeral in Michigan.

The family member was a brother-in-law who meant more to me than my own parents. His funeral was the fifth one I had attended in the previous nine months. The first was my sister's funeral, followed by my father-in-law's weeks later, and three months after that, my mother-in-law's. After that was the funeral of the brother of a close friend in the program, and then my brother-in-law. After thinking about all of the deaths, my attention widened to include other losses.

I thought of friends in the program who had gone out again; program friends who had died; meetings I had cherished that had changed or discontinued; medical bad news of several kinds that had hit my friends, my wife, and me, and so many things that had been necessary for me to accept to get on with my life and recovery. These were mountains I'd managed to climb, and it made me grateful for my growth in the program. Before recovery, the things over which I would stumble were mere bumps by comparison.

When I first experimented with the Serenity Prayer, when something crappy would happen, I would shoot straight for acceptance, attempting to do an end run around anger, hurt, and grief. As I had heard a sponsor say once to a sponsee, "You're trying to use the Serenity Prayer like a drug. It won't work. Before the healing comes the ouching."

Over the years, I have done some ouching, and some accepting. I learned that acceptance is not approval; it is simply recognizing the facts of reality: "That's the way it is." It's when I attempt to resist the facts of reality that my life becomes hell.

Today I am still engaged in that study of the Serenity Prayer. Everything that exists is either something I can change or something I cannot change. Curiously enough, all the things I find it necessary to accept are things I used to think I could change, while the things I find it necessary to change are things I used to think were carved in stone. Everything changes: the universe, life, and me.

111. It Started Out as a Joke

The god I was taught was a judgmental bastard that constantly poured over his accounting books, marking down my merits and demerits, measuring out the stretch of Hell I was to travel. As a child I would appeal to this spirit anytime I needed to feel guilty and ashamed. In the program I was taught that a higher power is whoever or whatever it is that you go to when you need help. For many of us a substance or behavior became our higher power: alcohol, pot, pills or other drugs, food, starvation, sex, gambling, religion, work, exercise, money, shopping, power, and others. Turning my will and my life over to drugs, gambling, and so on managed to bring me into rehab. Now what I needed was a higher power that would help me into recovery.

My first higher power was Whatever Works. Of course, when asked in group what my higher power was, after hearing my answer I would usually be asked, "Have you found anything yet that works?" And I hadn't until I made an enormous spiritual reach and went to my treatment group for help. That experiment worked, and I made the group my higher power—the thing I went to when I needed help.

After treatment I went back home to Maine, in the

process leaving behind in Minneapolis my "higher power." Again I was lost and desperate, with no one to whom I could turn, until I eventually found my way into a Twelve Step group and program and happily discovered that I had brought my higher power home with me in the form of my fellow recoverers. And that was what I had for a spiritual life for two years. If I had a problem, I'd share it at my meeting. More often than not, the answer to my problem would be at the meeting or would become clear to me soon afterwards. This eventually included the problem I was having with my higher power: the group. Using the group for a higher power became insufficient to fill my needs. The group wasn't with me except during meeting times, and the horrors, unfortunately, often come in the wee hours.

I took that problem to a meeting, but before I could share it with my program brothers and sisters, someone else shared the exact same problem. Before I knew what I was doing, out of my mouth leapt the following: "Since our group name is the Dragon-slayers, why not pick St. George for a higher power?" At the time, I thought I was making a joke.

Some months later I was back at my rehab attending a special workshop which treated the Al-Anon end of addiction. I attended with two sisters from my childhood family. The special program was for those affected by addiction in others, but who didn't have a relative going through rehab.

On the first day of this workshop I became terribly overwrought trying to work my older sister's program for her. I loved her dearly, and all I could see her doing was resisting recovery with all of the cynicism and bitterness at her considerable command. At last I blew up at her and was properly told by her to mind my own business.

I could not let it go. I went and saw my counselor, and she told me to mind my own business. "Barry," she said, "Do you mean to tell me that your sister's been in the program for four whole hours and she hasn't gotten to the place where you've gotten in two years?"

I still couldn't let it go. I went to an Al-Anon meeting that night, shared again what was bothering me, and was again advised to mind my own business. No one can work someone else's program. Everyone has to follow his or her own path, even if that path leads straight to destruction. "This is not a program for people who need it," someone said. "This is a program for people who want it."

Let it go. Let it go. But how? With another grueling day of workshops in front of me, at three o'clock the next morning I was sitting in bed in my room at the hospital still awake and still unable to let go. The irony was hard to bear. There I was, sitting in the bosom of my recovery, and I wanted to drink so badly I was about to explode. Again I did not know to whom or to what to turn. That was when I remembered the joke I had made about St. George. Suddenly the joke didn't seem so funny.

I was in enough pain to be willing to try anything, so I closed my eyes and asked St. George to help me to detach from how my sister was doing in the workshop and to help me go to sleep. The next thing I knew it was six in the morning and time to get up for breakfast, I was completely refreshed, and I had the ability to concentrate on my own program and otherwise mind my own business.

It is amazing how quickly I talked myself out of the spiritual experience I had witnessed firsthand. Tired, overwrought, I probably just pooped out from exhaustion. Why had I been completely refreshed after less than three hours of sleep? Who knew? How had I suddenly acquired the ability to let go and let my sister follow her own path? Well, that's what my counselor and those at the meeting told me to do, right? St. George and other ethereal higher powers were back to being jokes.

Six months later I again found myself with pain and with no one to whom I could turn. I was two and a half years into recovery and all I could think of was that I didn't have to be that miserable and sober, too. Again, through the encouragement of pain, I became willing to try anything.

I was driven to read some program literature. As I read, once more I faced the same thing I'd faced in rehab: If I wanted to recover from addiction, I would have to become willing to enlist the aid of a higher power of my own understanding.

It really went against the grain. It felt like such classic hypocrisy for me to pray to something in which I did not believe. Then I remembered something someone had said at a meeting: "For this program to work, you don't have to believe in it. All you have to do *is do it.*"

All of this was spinning in my head when I remembered my experience with St. George at the hospital a few months earlier. I sat on the edge of my bed, buried my face in my hands, and said, "I know you're bullshit, but are you really up there?"

I heard a voice, firm and clear: "It's about time you asked!"

The sense I got was of a benevolent power that had been waiting for a long time to help me, and that had gotten somewhat frustrated. I didn't devote the moment taking exception to this higher power's obvious petulance. Instead I began talking to this disembodied voice about how hard it had been the previous thirty months doing recovery mostly on my own. Imagination? Wishful thinking? Hallucination? Me talking to myself out of desperation? Who can say? I picked at it, doubted it, felt silly, and then felt a strong, gentle arm steal around my shoulders and hold me. I haven't felt alone since.

As someone once said, "It isn't the god you were taught that will save you. It is the god you will find."

112. Damn the Libidos! Full Speed Ahead!

There is a politically incorrect joke about the man who was trying to get his new mule to pull his wagon. He clucked, said "Giddyup," snapped the reins, begged, pleaded, and screamed. The mule would not move. A strapping young farm boy came walking along and the man said, "My mule won't go. Can you help me?"

"Sure," answered the farm boy. He turned, went to a scrap pile by the side of the road, and came back carrying a long two-by-four. The farm boy stood in front of the mule, took the two-by-four in hand like a baseball bat, and swung with all his might, smacking the mule upside his head. Putting down the lumber, he said to the man. "Now try it."

The man clucked at the mule and the mule began pulling the wagon. The man looked around at the farm boy and said, "I thank you, but why did that work?"

"First," the farm boy called out, "you have to get his attention!"

Although I do not advocate abusing mules with lengths of spruce, there are times in recovery, when observing the actions of newcomers, sponsees, or program mates destroying themselves, when my palms itch for the feel of a two-by-four. Okay, everybody has to work his or her own program, and there is no one sicker than the fellow who thinks he knows better than you how to run your program. There are times, though, when it is not only healthy but an act of love to remove one's silent consent to someone's up-and-coming disaster. Sometimes this is called "tough love."

There was one such incident I overheard next to the coffeepot during the break at a Twelve Step meeting. An old-timer was in the process of firing a sponsee. "For the life of me," said the old-timer, "I don't know why you asked me to be your sponsor. I don't think you've taken a single one of my suggestions. You don't do any of the Step work we agreed on, you never use the phone, you only hit a meeting every other blue moon, you're still hanging around with a bunch of drunks, and now you tell me you want to leave your wife and move in with a woman you just met last month at the student center. Don't you remember? No big changes in relationships for the first year of recovery. You must have heard it a thousand times?"

"Yes, but—"

"But nothing! For the life of me, kid, I don't know why you asked me to be your sponsor."

The young man looked quite contrite as he mouthed the program words, "I asked you to be my sponsor because I want what you have."

Responded the old-timer, "If you want what I have, you need to shop where I shop!"

113. For a Werewolf, Every Day Is a Bad-Hair Day

It was one of those days. Before I opened my eyes, I realized I hated my bed. It was too hard. I hated the bedroom, too. It didn't have enough windows, and the window it did have had a crappy view. Every noise from the highway outside seemed to be funneled onto my pillow, which had all of the comfort of a slab of granite. My back was sore, my love handles hadn't gotten any smaller, and I just couldn't face the thought of another session in front of the bathroom mirror watching my hairbrush grow hair faster than my head. I said to myself, "I haven't even gotten out of bed yet and the day is already in the toilet! What's going to happen when I get up and go to work?"

It was a bad day.

How bad was it?

It was so bad I was driven to call my sponsor, that's how bad it was. He invited me over to his house that evening, and he wasted no time. He sat me down at his kitchen table and said, "You've got GDA—Gratitude Deficiency Anemia. Here's how to do a gratitude list."

And he showed me. You take a piece of paper and run a line down the center. On the left side you write down your clean date. On the right side you write today's date. Returning to the left side, write down the names of all of the people you loved on your clean date, followed by the names of all of the people who loved you, then a list of all of the material things you had and how you felt about them. Finally, you write down how you felt then, about yourself, your purpose, and your place in the universe. After completing that, you do the same on the right side: In reference to today's date, you list those you love, those who love you, the material things you have and how you feel about them, and how you feel about yourself and your place in the universe today.

The left side was easy for me to fill out. On the day I got clean, I hated everyone, everyone was tired of me, and I either hated or was indifferent to the things I owned. How I felt about myself and my place in the universe was pretty well answered by having spent the two weeks prior to abstinence trying to figure out how to kill myself without making a mess.

When I turned my attention to the right side, I began with the names of the people I loved. I was at it for over an hour and hardly scratched the surface. There were dozens of people that I loved and dozens more that I felt loved me. I never got to the material possessions or my place in the universe. Actually, my place in the universe was just fine. I felt incredibly wealthy. I was grateful, which is the point.

The disease urges us to seek out the single fly speck on an otherwise clean wall and focus upon it until that fly speck expands and becomes the entire universe. Whenever I find myself in the midst of a bad-hair day, I try a gratitude list. It helps me to see beyond the fly speck.

114. The Wizards of Speed and Time

"A slow sort of country!" said the Queen. "Now, here, you see, it takes all the running you can do to keep in the same place. If you want to get somewhere else, you must run at least twice as fast as that!"
—Lewis Carroll, *Through the Looking Glass*

It was the main speaker's meeting at an NA convention and the fellow who was speaking had a hair-raising series of adventures to relate that were crazier *after* he had gotten clean than most of the drug war stories I've heard. During his first year clean, he continued to deal drugs, had a brush with organized crime that left him with a permanent limp, had two brushes with the police that left him on the run, went back to college, got married and divorced, bought a house and car, lost both, moved eleven times, made a try at becoming a rock star, and hopped spiritually from atheism to Mormonism, from Mormonism to Islam, and from Islam to Voodoo (I'm not certain all of this is accurate. I'm writing this from memory, and as I recall I took no notes. Instead, I just sat there with my mouth hanging open, twitching). The main theme of his talk, not surprisingly, was Easy does it.

"Many in early recovery run on full afterburners, trying to make up for the past," he said. "All too often the burnouts go out, back into the nightmare, once they discover that there is no way to make up for the past. In my case, I had a sponsor who managed to hold me down long enough to tell me the past was past. My choice was limited to what I was going to do in the present to stay clean and grow spiritually. He said the main thing I needed to do was to stop doing. I needed to slow down."

— ◆ —

Easy does it. Our life problems didn't all develop in one day and they can't all be resolved in one day. In addition, it makes no difference how fast we run. We cannot erase, recapture, or alter the past. Attempting to make up for lost time sets us up for failure.

"Well, how much should I slow down?" asked one road-burner at a meeting.

One suggestion was, "Take everything you're doing, cut it in half, then do half of the remainder."

Another suggestion was, "Keep slowing down until you can hear the traffic control instructions from your higher power."

There was a warning, though. "Don't keep slowing down until you're not working the program. The full slogan is Easy does it—but *do it!*"

115. We're Off to See the Wizard

In rehab my counselor used to say, "Our job here is to take soft heads and hard hearts and turn them into hard heads and soft hearts." It was her way of saying we were a bunch of thoughtless insensitive clods who might, with enough work, achieve the abilities to think things through and feel our feelings.

Thinking things through. That was something I always thought I did. Through working Step One, however, I learned about some amazing gaps in my thinking. Acts have consequences. The one doing the act is responsible for the consequences of that act. If I pick up a drug, intending to use only one, I am going to use many more than one. I am, therefore, responsible for picking up the first one and all that follow. If I don't want to go off on a life-threatening tear, I simply do not pick up the first one, which means doing all that I need to do to avoid picking up that first one. Thinking things through.

Feeling my feelings. That was also something I thought I already did. I was depressed or angry all the time, wasn't I? Through working Step One and Step Four, though, I learned that there was a whole range of feelings that were never allowed to be felt: fear, happiness, and love among them. Fear was the one, curiously enough, that frightened me the most. I learned, however, that I really had been feeling fear throughout my using years. It was just that it came out as anger, rage, depression, and humor. Humor? That's right, I literally laughed my way through a lifetime of horrors committed by me and against me. It took all I could scrape together to allow these feelings to be felt, which is why, years later, I laughed so hard at a conversation I overheard.

It was after a Twelve Step meeting and a newcomer was in the process of trying on her first sponsor. She asked the old-timer, "What will I need to stay clean?"

"Do you have a Basic Text?"

"Yes."

"Do you have telephone numbers?"

"Yes."

"What about a meeting list?"

The newcomer held up the booklet. "I have a meeting list."

Her sponsor nodded and said, "Then all you have

to do is go to the Emerald City and see the Wizard of Oz."

"What?"

The old-timer smiled. "The only things you're missing are a heart, courage, and a brain."

116. Picking Life

Every moment of every day is filled with life and death choices for me. It's easy to see these choices as life and death when the decision is whether to pick up that drink, drug, or cigarette. It's almost as easy to see life and death choices in making another bet or pigging out at a picnic. It's often almost impossible, however, to see the choices as between life and death when the decision is between forgiveness or resentment.

I hooked up to a machine and checked it out. Resentment increases stress, which has all kinds of health consequences, ranging from heart disease to possibly some forms of cancer. Having a resentment is like picking up a hammer, smacking myself in the head, and saying to the object of my resentment, "There! Take that!" Resentment isn't something I do to someone else; it's something I do *to myself.*

Then isn't it curious that so much of my time is taken up with resentments? Actually, it's not curious at all. For a lot of my lifetime I believed that resentment was my only way of asserting myself, of striking back. Confrontation, setting boundaries, and letting go were forms of insanity. In full-blown addiction, every resentment was dragon fuel. The dragon, therefore, helped arrange my life so that I had plenty of causes to have resentments, and made it so every resentment became set in cement.

Acquiring, exercising, feeding, and polishing resentments is automatic for me. To forgive I have to take action. I have to do the hardest work that there is for me to do: I must grow spiritually. But do I stay locked into the health-threatening misery of resentment, or do I choose life? This would look like a no-brainer, but I often astonish myself with the number of times I choose resentment and death.

For today I am aware of my choices and their consequences, and today I choose life.

117. By the Light of the Blue Flame

There are zealots in recovery whose enthusiasm takes forms that make program officers look like wimps in comparison. They have been likened to having blue flames shooting from their asses, and last night I tangled with the blue flamer from hell. Nothing I did in the program was right, I had nothing to offer, my clean time was nothing, my program was a sham, and my life in recovery was a waste. His way was *the* way, and he was bound and determined to show me the error of my ways.

What was sick on my part, in reflection, was sitting there defending myself. I had an ulterior motive, however. In my program youth, the spark of my spiritual awakening beneath me, I had burned some methane of my own. I know that five or ten years from now, if the blue flamer is still in recovery, he will have mellowed somewhat. A spiritual awakening sits differently on you as time in recovery increases. If it doesn't, there is no growth.

In addition, blue flamers have a lot to offer, beginning with passion and enthusiasm. Tireless carriers of the message, they often get others caught up in their enthusiasm long enough to give recovery a good try. By the same token, this my-way-or-the-highway attitude often chases some away—newcomers and old-timers alike. This is why we have Tradition Four, "Each group should be autonomous except in matters affecting other groups or [AA, NA, OA, etc.] as a whole."

So I sat there trying to save the blue flamer's enthusiasm while introducing some tolerance of other ways of doing recovery into the equation. In other words, I was trying to change him and he was trying to change me. There is no sicker or more pointless way for program people to spend their time. What we both needed, actually, was a meeting with our respective support group.

When I got home after this emotional workout, it was late and my head was caught in a twister. Intellectually, I know what my recovery means to me; and how HP, the program, and I worked together to achieve it. I know a lot of the men, women, and children I have helped, and there are many more I don't even know I have helped. Yet there was still this little voice in my head saying, "Gotcha! That's it, you fraud! You've been found out! Your recovery is nothing! Your life is all waste."

Actually, it wasn't such a little voice. It was a pretty damned big voice. That was when I remembered an unmade amend of mine from my Step Eight list of impossible amends. I was twenty years old, in the army, and was shooting my own blue flames. There were a number of us on a police detail picking up cigarette butts. I was doing what I usually did in such circumstances: whining. I was a school-trained missile technician, made so by the expenditure of many thousands of taxpayer dollars, and here the army had me—*me*—on a bloody police call! Where was the sense? Where was the justice?

The sergeant who was in charge of the detail was in his fifties, and he was a rather cheerful man who made the mistake of trying to jolly me out of my shitty attitude. He made some comment about someone listening to me might get the impression that I didn't like the army.

I stood up, looked at him, and let the blue flames fly. I said, "Sarge, it's just that when I'm fifty I hope I'm going to be good for something more than just picking up cigarette butts."

Talk about your off-the-cuff, instant invalidation. This guy was a combat veteran, an electronics technician, a family man, and successful in that he was a soldier and happy with the work he was doing and the life he was leading. What's more, police call is just the army's way of doing some housekeeping. No soldier's life comes down to doing nothing but picking up butts. But, in essence, that's what I told him his life was.

I suppose if that sergeant had been as healthy and as self-confident as I wish I had been, he could have passed the whole thing off as one asshole's opinion. But I saw his face. I told him his life was shit, and he had one of those not-so-little voices inside of him that said to him, "Gotcha! That's it, you fraud. You've been found out!"

As soon as I saw his face, I regretted what I had said. I didn't say that, though. I just went back to picking up the butts, but this time with my mouth shut. I don't know if he remembers the incident, or if he's still alive, but it has bothered me ever since. I do not know anyone well enough to condemn and scorn his or her life. I know all too little of the things that brought me to where I am today. I have almost none of this information about another. This is why my judgment about another's life is worthless. As with all those others I cannot find to whom I owe amends, perhaps you'll find this, Sarge, and accept my apology.

Still, there was the problem of my own blue flamer, and that voice inside me who calls me a fraud. I prayed and asked the universe to tell me what I needed to know right then. There were two answers. The first was that defeat does not lie in trying and failing; defeat lies in failing to try. The second was to accept people for exactly what they are, including the blue flamer—and me.

Today I hold before me a truth that I have seen proven many hundreds of times over the years: in the program there is no limit to the number of paths to recovery and spirituality. The power we appeal to, regardless of the name, shapes itself and its help to each of us as individuals. We are individuals, and that is why we are told "It's an individual program." I need to throw in, as well, that my calling someone else judgmental is being judgmental. Everyone is exactly where he or she is supposed to be.

118. What Is Recovery?

Recovery is the condition of having recovered. With an injury or disease, recovering means returning to a state of health. When we're talking about any of the addictions, compulsions, and obsessions treated by Twelve Step programs, we're talking about diseases; and therefore recovering means returning to a state of health. Of course, this presumes one was healthy at some time in the past. Many of us with mothers who were addicts were born addicted. And those who grew up in alcoholic homes never had a stretch of mental health to which they can return. Instead of "re-covering," perhaps people like us should call the reach for health simply "covering."

We've heard it a thousand times at meetings and from sponsors: "We have a disease that affects us physically, mentally, and spiritually." Recovery or health, then, means becoming healed in these three areas. The standard of what constitutes physical health is the concern of physicians. Mental health is the concern of headshrinkers and wig-pickers. And spiritual health? In the program it seems as though everyone and his or her third cousin have appointed themselves experts in this area. I recently heard recovery defined as follows: "I think recovery is spending every moment trying to get closer to God and seeking his will." This was fine, for him. What was not fine for me is when he concluded with, "If you are not spending every moment trying to get closer to God, you are not in recovery."

Addiction for me was slavery. Recovery for me is freedom. One part of freedom for me is not enslaving myself—becoming obsessed—about service to a particular conception of a higher power. That, to me, is little more than swapping one disease for another. But, then, what is spiritual recovery?

When I was young in the program, this subject came up at a meeting, and the speaker was filled with passion and conviction. He laid down what recovery was, and if anyone else thought differently, they were not in recovery. Since what he was talking about was not even remotely what I wanted for my life, I was just a little panicked. I had a long talk about this with my sponsor.

He began by pointing out that some persons handle being without drugs by becoming Wednesday night messiahs. "Every human is unique, and that uniqueness rests in his or her spirituality. Recovery is becoming who you were meant to be. It's *your* recovery. Don't ever let someone else pick out for you who you will become." Then we went on to spiritual health.

First, he wanted to know what my symptoms of spiritual sickness were when I was using. There was a suicide attempt. It spoke to many things regarding my spiritual condition. I hated myself, I hated the world and everything in it, and I had no hope that things would or could get any better. There was nothing I wanted that I didn't hate once I got it, and life to me was a curse.

Thanks to being clean and sober, and to a lot of work with sponsors, the Steps, and counselors, I continually move closer to loving myself. The world is now filled with persons, critters, and things I love. In addition, I have hope and confidence in the future. For me this is recovery, and we haven't even gotten around to the subject of higher powers.

The difference between god-obsession and spiritual recovery has been pointed out before: in my (admittedly biased) opinion, religion is for those who don't want to go to Hell. Spirituality is for those who have already been to Hell and don't want to go back.

For me recovery is freedom, and freedom is the infinite palette of choices available to each of us as to the forms our individual recoveries might take, whether it be dedicating one's life to a higher power, to a sport, an ideal, a love, or to an end to needless suffering. For today, life is a very precious gift, and it feels like recovery to me.

119. The F-Word

"Family is the F-Word." The woman at the support group meeting was shaking her head in disbelief and frustration. "In the program I've learned how to detach with love from my alcoholic husband and my addicted son. When the disease is working them, they can both be mean-mouthed. They say and do some of the most horrible and hurtful things. Then I remember it's the disease talking, to loathe the behavior but love the person. When the venom comes at me at high speed, I remember to put up my shit shield. That I can do this is a miracle for which I am very grateful." She took a deep breath and I distinctly heard the sounds of teeth grinding together. "With my mother, however, it's a whole different story. All she has to do is raise a bloody eyebrow at me and I go berserk!"

Our family members have access to a whole different set of buttons, all of them wired into little bombs beneath our self-worth, confidence, and serenity. If someone in the program, for example, accuses me of something, I can detach, look at the accusation to see if it has any merit, and then either act to correct the matter or let go of it. All my mother had to do was do this little tooth-sucking thing she used to do to show her irritation and immediately I became the Wicked Witch of the West crying, "I'm melting! I'm melting!"

"I don't have to prove anything to anyone," said an old-timer. "Yet when my brother talked behind my back and accused me of something dishonest,

I was in a scramble to fix it, change his mind, prove to him that he was wrong. No matter what I did, though, I couldn't change his mind a single bit. What I got from it was headaches, back problems, and hives. What I learned from that experience is that there is no surer way to shatter your serenity than to try and change someone else."

Among the many things no one can change is his or her biological origin. No matter how sick or fragmented, we are issued a family at birth, even if it's no more than an orphanage. We didn't get to pick our families, and one of the devils that often follows us into recovery is trying to make our families into what they should have been.

Once in recovery, I suddenly had all of these answers. Shortly thereafter a vision appeared before me. It was what life could be like if everyone in my family got into recovery. Talk about your unrealistic expectations.

"Anytime you think your serenity is going too well," a sponsor once told me, "make it a personal priority to change someone else."

So how do I detach with love from the toxic, guilt-flinging members of my own family? Acceptance of others as who, where, and what they were and are is the answer. And how do I do that? For myself I needed some physical separation. This was no problem with the ones who died of addiction. With them the task began with grieving all of the fantasy might-have-beens, having several good cries and lousy days, and then focusing on reality: what was and what is. It began with accepting that my mother was a monster, then amending that to accepting she was a very sick woman who acted like a monster, then amending it once more to accepting that I really didn't know her at all. The only thing I got to know was her disease.

With the members of my family still living, I pretty much had to accept that my disease and theirs made it so that they didn't know me and I didn't know them. My job? To remain open enough to find out who and what each of them is. If there is love, respect, and open-mindedness, I remain open. If there is humiliation, criticism, blaming, and hateful attacks, I have to increase the distance.

Yes, that is very sad. It's not anywhere near as damaging, however, as constantly flogging myself with how things should have been, or the even sicker effort to make the past into something other than what it was. Often pain is the price of healing, and accepting reality for what it was and is can be painful. But I let it go. I write about it, work the Steps, stuff it in my god box, and look with gratitude at all of the family members I can choose in the program. And if a member of my biological family should reach for the kind of help I can give, I'll be there.

—◆—

Today I will make taking care of myself my first priority. Unless I am in recovery, I can be of help to no one else.

120. HOW

In general there are three types of hard cases that make it through the doors of recovery: atheists, God-haters, and followers of various religions. To work the Twelve Steps of Recovery, all three need to change. The atheist doesn't need to believe in "God," but does need to choose and use a higher power of some sort. That's in the Steps. For the same reason, the God-hater doesn't need to love "God," but does need a higher power. The religionist doesn't need to throw out his or her religion, but does need to bring his or her religious notions into rehab, because the existing ones obviously weren't working.

Raising this subject, of course, is sort of like spreading oil on troubled fires. The HOW of recovery, though, is Honesty, Open-mindedness, and Willingness. With that in mind we sit down before our blank sheet of paper to create the power that will give us the guidance and strength we need to enter and grow in recovery.

Create this power?

I remember asking, "If I have the ability to create this power, then why don't I have this power myself?"

Keep it simple. Those who want to recover do not need to know how many angels can stand on a pinhead. (If the pinhead is a certain guy I know, we are talking a heap of angels!) In any event, we are not creating this higher power. Instead we are opening ourselves to allow "it"—something—into our lives. All we need at this stage of recovery is a power that can restore us to sanity. Curiously enough, we don't need to know much about either the power or the sanity for a higher power to work for us.

Honesty, Open-mindedness, Willingness.

"Go ahead. Pick something for a higher power."

"That's silly."

"It may be silly, but it works."

"If I'm going to do this, I need something I believe in, at least a little."

Honesty, Open-mindedness, Willingness. This is the attitude that brought everything I needed to know within range. I began with something I didn't believe in at all, but I tried to be honest about myself and what I needed. I used my mental crowbar to keep my mind open to the answers I needed, and all of this was fueled by a willingness to reach out and find that new way of life called recovery. As each year in recovery passed, I saw that my higher power, my understanding of it, and its benefits to me continually changed. I saw, too, that my belief in it changed, as well. With each passing moment I appreciated more and more the miracle of my own recovery, the miracles of those I love who are in recovery, and the countless miracles of this army of the recovering around the world.

Today I will remember that the answers I seek and need are there and will present themselves to me as I increase my knowledge about how HOW works.

121. HP Mart

A sponsee once told me, "When you tell me to pick up a pencil and pick and choose the things that make up my higher power, it sounds like there ought to be a super celestial department store out there: HP Mart."

After thinking on it a good while, I answered, "You're right. There is."

It's funny how all of the learned treatises and profound writings I have explored for enlightenment over the years didn't come together in my mind until someone new in the program made a joke to express his confusion. Here is a description of one such super celestial department store. There are others, but this is the one where I do my shopping:

Modern physics tells us that the universe, which is all that exists, is made up of energy, intelligence, and information. This matrix is such that it is impossible to alter one part of this matrix without changing in some manner every other part of the entire matrix. For one example, if I alter one part of the matrix by asking for help, it affects every part of the entire matrix, and the help I need comes. Does that mean if I ask for a million dollars, I get it? First I need to know if the help I need is the million dollars.

Still, in a process called visualization, people in sports and business for years have been utilizing this power to achieve their goals. In their minds they "see" themselves performing certain acts, taking particular steps, achieving particular goals. Enough of these goals have been achieved over time to prove that visualization works, which is why so many persons in business and sports use this technique. Another name for visualization is "prayer." Another name for this vast matrix of energy, intelligence, and information is "God" or higher power.

The implications of this are enormous, especially when we look at Carl Jung's theories concerning the "unconscious." In his introduction to Jung's *Man and His Symbols* (Doubleday, 1964), John Freeman wrote, "In Jung's view the unconscious is the great guide, friend, and adviser of the conscious. . . ."

The universe is all that exists, which makes us all parts of the universe. I can send my intentions, desires, or prayers into this matrix of energy, intelligence, and information, and there is a part of me, what Jung calls the unconscious, that receives instructions from the matrix and tries like hell to pass this information on to me (my conscious). To get this mechanism to work for me, I need to know ever more about myself and to open communication between my self and this friendly other self. The potential power of the entire universe is there to help me, which is certainly enough to help me in recovery. What's more, there is no conception of a higher power I have either heard of or thought of that isn't some small part of this incomprehensible whole.

"God [or higher power], who is the universe, of which we are all parts . . ." is how I begin my "prayers" or messages to the universe. And I listen to the messages I receive. It works for me, and it shows why, no matter what kind or form of higher power you choose, it will work as long as you use it. Your higher power is different from mine? That's cool. They all work.

Still, it is the act of reaching for help that brings the help we need, more than exactly who or what we reach. It has happened to me dozens of times: I need help, I phone my sponsor or someone else, and no one is in, yet I get the help I need. Every time we ask for help, our higher powers hear, and the help comes.

By the time we stumble through the doors into the program, we are usually wrung out spiritually. It is easier to get a gallon of AB negative from a turnip than faith from a newcomer one day off his or her substance or behavior. That's why Twelve Step programs are action programs, not faith programs. As some crusty folks keep pointing out, "Keep it simple. You don't have to believe in this shit for it to work. All you have to do is *do it*."

122. I Couldn't Sleep at All Last Night

I call them three-in-the-morning pillow-burners. The head gets started pulling on a thread, eventually unraveling the night's sleep. How can it be? I read in bed at night until I'm nodding off, I turn off the light, and let the night train take me. Then at midnight, one, two, or three in the morning, I awaken with my brain chewing on something I should have said, would have said, if only I'd done, or countless little scenarios of future conversations or letters that will never see the light of day, sanity willing.

If I don't get a full night's sleep I'm going to be cranky and grouchy all the next day. So, I *must* get back to sleep. There is, of course, nothing in the world that can keep me awake quite as well as trying with all my might to fall asleep. Old injuries and humiliations float through my head, a current disagreement, a resentment or two, if only this hadn't happened, if only that had happened—the next thing I know I'm dancing all over the past and future.

What I used to do back in the bad old days was to pop a few sleeping pills and maybe follow it with a beer or three. I would have no problem getting back to sleep. Curiously enough, I was cranky and grouchy the next day nonetheless. Not only that, there was the morning challenge of not having my head roll off my shoulders into the toilet.

When I got out of rehab I had this sleep problem—there wasn't enough of it. At best I would get half an hour of sleep, then I was up. I would lie there for hours, twiddling my thumbs, counting resentments jumping over a fence, and generally getting frantic. The next morning I'd go into my office, sit down to work, and all I could do was look groggily at my computer monitor and mutter curses. That night, ragged and tired, I'd fall right off to sleep. Then, half an hour later, I'd wake up and burn more holes in my pillow.

I brought my dilemma to a meeting. One fellow, a physician who was addicted to the same drugs I had used, shared that the drugs had knocked my internal sleep timers out of whack. Once I had completely detoxed, things would change. In time, it would correct itself.

"What do I do until then?" I asked.

"Tough it out. No one ever died from a lack of sleep."

"I'm not worried about dying," I answered. "I'm concerned about committing murder."

An old-timer in the back of the room said, "Look for the opportunity in the situation."

Look for the opportunity!

I had a flash fantasy concerning this old-timer at the bottom of a well filled with flaming oil. "Why don't you look for the opportunity in that!" I'd shout.

That night, my eyes wide open, I remembered the suggestion. Look for the opportunity. Well, let's face it. I had been given a gift of eight extra hours a day. I got up and began filling in that eight hours with things I wanted to do. Writing, remodeling my office, reading; I also took up wood carving, where I learned a lot about patience and how to use a tourniquet.

I remember waking up my wife at three in the morning as my cut finger was pumping out the scarlet billows. "Is the cut deep?" she asked, her eyes wide.

"No," I answered confidently, "the bone stopped it."

It's amazing how much work you can get done if you're putting in a twenty-four-hour shift. The writing became a book of mine about a group of patients who go through a rehab. The book subsequently sold, was published, and helped and entertained a lot of readers. My office was completely remodeled with pine paneling, new light fixtures, new rug, and air conditioning that I ran into the rest of the house through ducts that I made myself. My wood carvings have won art awards, and I have even sold quite a few of them. And after about six months, my internal clock began its repairs, and I started to sleep again, which also has its opportunities.

Tonight, if I can't sleep, I'll look for the opportunity and put the time to good use. And tomorrow I'll take what catnaps I can.

123. The Three Ms of Recovery

The first time I heard it was in rehab: "No big changes in love relationships for at least the first year of recovery. This means no moving out, moving in, divorcing, marrying, or anything else. In early recovery things are very confused, and you need to know what you have before you change it for something else."

There is another reason I heard at a meeting one night when the topic was, once again, relationships. The unhappy fellow who was sharing pointed out that when he sobered up, he had no one at all. Why does he have to do without for a year?

"Before there can be a 'we' relationship," answered an old-timer, "you first need to find out who *you* are."

The unhappy one squirmed, turned red, and said, "Yeah, but what about . . . you know . . . sex? Am I supposed to become a monk?"

"What you need," said another newcomer, "are the three Ms of recovery: meetings, meditation, and masturbation."

There are good reasons for that thinking. Many of us used other persons as drugs, obsessing about a relationship and trying to control it. Others of us used relationships as nests that enabled us to remain insane. On my one-year anniversary, I was on a return visit to the rehab I attended. There was a young man in my group who was also on his one-year return visit. He looked and acted like he was on his first day in recovery. He eventually shared about what he had done for the past year.

Three weeks out of rehab, he began dating a woman who was not in the program. Shortly after that, he moved in with her and they lived together, not quite happily ever after. His entire world became centered on this woman, and everything else—meetings, the Steps, recovery, a job—fell by the wayside. He hadn't used any addictive substances—just a person. It made no difference, for the results were the same. He was still beating his head bloody against the starting gate.

The facts are these: to make it into any Twelve Step program one has to be an emotional cripple. It's a course prerequisite. Emotionally healthy people don't come through the program doors because they don't need the program. Before any kind of healthy love relationship can exist, there is much healing and emotional growth that needs to take place. Getting into a new love relationship in early recovery is unfair to the other person and is guaranteed to be a disaster to the one trying to recover.

At another Twelve Step meeting, on the same topic, I heard, once again, the three Ms of recovery: meetings, meditation, and masturbation. "But what if I get addicted to it?" asked the desperate soul.

"There's a Twelve Step program for that, too," answered one of the program brothers. "They give out the same advice there as they do here in any Twelve Step meeting: don't pick up, go to meetings, and ask for help."

124. That's Your Higher Power Talking to You

It had been a week since I had been roasted at a meeting by a pack of blue flamers who had discovered the light and the truth and were bound and determined that their way was the only way and that I was the great Satan standing in the way of universal nirvana. Despite the passage of time, I hadn't quite figured out what to do with the experience. I had learned some things. First, two people spending hours angrily trying to argue each other into changing makes about as much sense as if they stood there toe-to-toe smacking the crap out of each other with cricket bats.

I learned something else, as well. That little voice inside of me that tells me I'm a fraud is dead wrong, and so are the blue flamers who attempt to conjure this demon within me. Since the experience was still troubling me, however, I knew there was more to learn. There I was at the site of the episode listening to one of the witnesses describe her feelings of fear and outrage about what happened. When she was finished, and after another member expressed her gratitude at not having been at that particular meeting, a visitor spoke up.

He shared that at one time in his early recovery, there was this one meeting in his home area that he really hated. The reason he hated it was that there was this one person who was the group's self-appointed guru and who always chaired every meeting. Not only that, he would comment at length upon the sharing of others at the meeting, offering his pearls of wisdom and lumps of advice in the process. Most of every meeting was taken up with this fellow's monologues, and it used to drive our visitor nuts.

"I really hated that guy. Whenever I'd go to that meeting, all I could think of as this jerk interrupted everyone to hand out his advice was how much he pissed me off. I talked with my sponsor about this guy and how much I hated him. My sponsor said to me, 'Either he'll change or he'll get high.' Then he added, 'Either you'll change or you'll get high.'

"And he was right. Neither of us changed and we both got high."

In the back of my head I heard myself say to myself: "That's your higher power talking to you."

An astonishingly high number of program blue flamers and program officers I've known eventually either changed or went back to using; mellowed out or went out. The rest of them are out in the minefield riding pogo sticks. The relapse rangers I've known who couldn't forgive an injury or let go of a resentment could fill a small stadium.

Acceptance.

Everyone is exactly where they're supposed to be.

That means all of them, and also thee and me.

Dear God, grant me the serenity to let assholes be assholes.

Pray for them.

Let go.

A Thaves cartoon clarified the matter for me. It shows a rather disreputable looking rabbit sitting at a bar, an open bottle before him, a tumbler of booze clutched in his paw. As the rabbit stares off into the distance, his face is crowded with an angry frown. The bartender rabbit is saying to him, "For Heaven's sake, *forget* about the tortoise!"

125. The ABCs of Addiction

Addiction comes with a philosophy, complete with ethics. It's called the ABCs of Addiction: Always be cool. If no one can see I've got a problem, then maybe I don't have a problem. Appearances are always more important than substance, problems will take care of themselves as long as I don't look at them, and never do today what you can put off until some other time. What is even more interesting, is that no one in the universe looks and acts less cool than an addict into his or her substance or behavior of choice. The first evidence of this that I noticed took place about a year before I went into treatment.

Because of my profession, I often attend conventions put on by readers and media fans, and at some of these happenings the writer's organization to which I belong will have a hospitality suite with free booze for all the writers and their guests. For some curious reason, it was at such hospitality suites where I used to hang out.

At one such event, I was sitting in a comfortable chair talking with another author about business, art, and the events of the day. While he nursed his drink, I would get up every now and then to refill my glass from the beer keg at the bar. The discussion proceeded, and I was just congratulating myself on finally acquiring some social skills, when a very loud crash came from the other end of the room in which we were sitting. I got up and walked over to find out the cause of the noise.

What I saw was beer spilled all over the floor and a young man—a newly published writer—passed out on the shattered remains of a coffee table. He was definitely down for the count. "What happened?" I asked.

A friend of mine put down his own tankard and said, "I don't know for sure, Barry. An hour ago, though, he told me that he was going to start matching you drink for drink."

I looked at my watch and felt slightly troubled. It wasn't just the implication that I might have a reputation as a drinker as well as an unusual tolerance for alcohol. What really bothered me was that I had been drinking for two hours or so before the kid began his experiment.

Always be cool.

How little this attitude changed when, clean and sober, I was in the program. It was still important to be cool. All that changed was the standard of appearance. I became a walking Rolodex of program sayings, pieces of wisdom, and fictional life experiences to relate—what Bill W. used to refer to as "parables"— and I was parabling my ass off. Who or what do I have to become to be cool? I was well on my way to becoming a group guru when somebody else's sponsor pulled me aside after a meeting and said, "You know, Barry, your job here isn't to convince everyone that you are recovered. Your job is to recover."

It's scary finding out that you are as transparent as a pane of glass. I had seen it a hundred times with others as they did numbers on themselves, but I couldn't see it in myself. That's why I'm blind without my program family. If I am not hiding behind my cool, though, what will people see?

Me?

Now, that's *really* scary.

126. Expect a Mackerel

There is a bumper sticker that says, "Expect a Miracle." It is a well-intentioned effort to remind us all that our continued recoveries depend upon miracles happening in our lives. Certainly the miracles happen. The problem comes with expecting the miracle. To expect it, we necessarily have to choose its form. Perhaps we coax ourselves into expecting forgiveness from someone we've injured, a wad of money, a promotion, a new love relationship, burning bushes in the living room, guest appearances by spirits, or the final removal of all our problems. When the expected miracle fails to materialize, our disappointment often hides the real miracles.

Recently I made my annual pilgrimage to a local Twelve Step convention. Not coincidentally, the name of the convention is The Miracle. I had had a number of deaths in my family over the past year, and other problems that were weighing me down. I was beginning to wonder what in the hell had happened to my miracle, when I heard others sharing. Incidentally, I was listening extra hard because I still had around twenty thousand words to come up with for this book. It is amazing how much more I hear when I am actually listening. That's why a radio works better when it's tuned in.

In any event, as I listened I heard the pain from a number of men and women who had lost loved ones—family and program—during the preceding twelve months. In addition, there were life-and-death problems concerning health, children, and other issues. Somewhere in the midst of all of this pain, the glorious size of the miracle suddenly burst into my awareness: *we were all still clean.*

Think about it: a bunch of addicts who, before the program, couldn't make it through a day or two without numbing their feelings over such weighty problems as a flat tire or the coming of Monday, facing and dealing with such things as death and devastating loss *without using.* The miracle was there, but I hadn't expected it.

Expectations are attempts to control the future. "Here's what's going to happen," and an entire framework of fabricated events and conclusions becomes part of our imagined reality. When things don't go according to our projections, we become disappointed to devastated, and the dragon begins to drool. That's why they say, "Plan, don't project." My job is to make the effort. Outcomes are not within my power. And miracles? I know that I am living one right now and that more will come as I need them. The time? The type? The form? I don't know. That's not my department. That's why, when they tell me, "Expect a miracle," I tell them, "No. It's 'Expect a mackerel, but keep the tuna handy, just for the halibut.'"

127. It's Not a Disease of Stupid People, But . . .

Baffled.

Absolutely stumped.

I was trying to turn my basement into a recreation room complete with fully stocked bar. I could easily envision myself as the bartender graciously serving my many guests and entertaining them with my brilliance and wit. What I could not figure out was how to finish off the bleeding basement.

I would have a beer in my hand, I'd go down the basement stairs, sit on a bucket, and try and figure it out. It was the ceiling that was the enigma. I wanted to put a pine ceiling up there, but before I could do that, there were some plumbing and heating pipes that needed to be raised. Before I could raise them, though, there were portions of the floor that looked as though they had dry rot and needed replacement. Also, the house was built with hand-hewn beams of no great beauty, many of which were roundish and covered with bumps and dips. Before I could do anything about them, there was some ancient wiring that needed to be brought up to code, and somewhere I had to get a copy of the code, and before that . . .

Before that, I would open another beer, then another, and another, until I would turn off the lights because I couldn't stand looking at this impossible project another minute. I would spend hours, sitting there in the dark, drinking, absolutely baffled. Why couldn't I even get moving on the basement?

There was another thing that had me stumped. I was drinking too much rum and whiskey, so I switched to beer. My weight started shooting up, so I switched to light beer. I was saving an enormous number of calories with diet beer. Three six-packs of sixteen-ounce cans. That's over a thousand calories a day! Why wasn't I losing any weight?

And then I got into the program, and bit by little bit the fog started to clear. I was still baffled, however. Only the subject changed. Why do I need a higher power? What good is a sponsor going to do me?

Then more fog cleared. Still, I hear those familiar voices in the halls:

"How did the accident happen?"

"I don't know, man. I threw up while I was driving my car. I turned on my windshield wipers, but I still couldn't see."

—◆—

A sponsee to his sponsor: "Why do you want me to work the Steps? They're for those with learning disabilities."

"That's right!" answered his sponsor.

—◆—

Overheard at an AA meeting: "You know, heroin can lead to a slip."

—◆—

Overheard at an NA meeting: "It's very hard to stay clean when you're using."

—◆—

Overheard at an OA meeting: "When I reach a year of abstinence from compulsive overeating, I'm going to binge out on chocolate until I see brown!"

Her sponsor's eyebrows went up. "That would be like an alcoholic celebrating her first year of sobriety by getting drunk."

"Yeah," the sponsee responded. "What's your point?"

—◆—

And there was the recovering drug addict who brought his problem and placed it before the meeting: "See, I've got a lot of big bills and I still can't find a job. I need the money, so is it okay for me to go back dealing drugs? I won't use the money to buy drugs; just to pay my bills. How about it?"

As we watched his sponsor pick up a two-by-four and drag him off to the coffee room, we call out the usual: "Keep coming back." It's the program way of saying, "Are you outta your goddamned mind?"

128. No Stupid Questions

An apocryphal tale:

A young man, new in the program, was out ice fishing, and he wasn't having much luck. No matter what he did he didn't seem to be able to catch anything. Only twenty feet away at another hole, an old man was fishing and was pulling them in one after another. The newcomer thought a moment and remembered his sponsor telling him that there are no stupid questions. If you don't know something, take a risk and ask. The kid went over to the old man and said, "I'm not catching anything and here you are only twenty feet away catching one after another. What do I need to do?"

"Ga ocha eep ga urnor," mumbled the old man.

"What?" asked the kid. "I didn't understand."

"Ga ocha eep ga urnor!" the old man repeated.

"I'm sorry," said the kid. "I still don't understand."

The old man spat on the ice and said, "You got to keep your worms warm."

There are few things quite as frightening as being the new kid in the program, unless it's being the new kid in the Army or in the penitentiary. Everyone seems to know what to do and what's going on, and the last thing the newcomer wants to do is look uncool by appearing ignorant. It's strange when you think about it. It's only by running out of answers that we make it through the doors into the halls of recovery, where we immediately take on the appearance of having all the answers.

Vulnerability is letting down the walls that separate me from those around me. After a past of injury and betrayal, nothing seemed quite as stupid as becoming vulnerable, but I had to lower those walls a bit if the life-saving information I needed was going to get in. When I was new in the program, though, appearances were everything. The reason is simple. To my mind, appearances were all I had left.

So many important questions: How do I stay away from the stuff? What is a sponsor? What is letting go? Where are more meetings? What's a higher power? Why do I need any of this stuff?

Then the tougher questions: Will you be my sponsor? Higher power, are you really up there? Can you help me? Will you help me? Am I worth recovery?

And then the really tough questions: Who was I? What was I? Who and what am I now? How can I become what I was meant to be? What am I meant to be?

If I want to get better, I need to ask for help. As long as I remain the only source for this information, I remain my own higher power, and I'll keep getting the same old disastrous answers.

—◆—

Sponsor to sponsee: "What's the difference between you and God?"

"I don't know. What's the difference between me and God?"

"God doesn't think he's you."

129. Exact Change, Please

Most of us are about as eager to be changed as
we were to be born, and go through our changes
in a similar state of shock.

—James Baldwin

I heard it for the first time in rehab: "To recover you
are going to have to change everything but your hair
color, unless changing your hair color will help; then
change that, too."

How I live, why I live, how I work, why I work, what
I work at, who I have for friends, why I have friends,
how I think, what I think, why I think, relationships,
morals, sex, goals, love, hope, charity . . .

Looked at in its entirety, the list of my changes is
staggering. They did not happen all at once, though,
and they are not completed by any stretch of the
imagination. I am a work in progress. Sometimes,
however, the progress is slow, as is illustrated by the
following doubtful history.

There was a first sergeant in the Army who had
a reputation for drinking and for having all of the
sensitivity of a cluster bomb in a hemorrhoid clinic.
One day his company commander came out of his
office and said to the first sergeant, "I just got word
that Private Jones's mother has passed away. Let him
know, and let him down easy."

"Yessir," answered the topkick. "I'll take care of
it."

At chow time, the first sergeant falls in the company, takes reports, reads the announcements and orders for the day, then calls out, "Private Jones?"

"Yes, sergeant?"

"Your mother dropped dead. Company dismissed!"

The captain was horrified at this treatment, and decided to take action. He ordered the first sergeant to go into the Army's Twelve Step rehabilitation program, which stressed sensitivity training. The sergeant went to rehab, stopped drinking, and got sensitive. A few weeks later, the captain said to the topkick, "It's Private Evans. His mother has passed away. Now, I want you to let him down easy, understand?"

"Yessir. I know what I did wrong before and I'll take care of it. Don't you worry."

At chow time the first sergeant falls in the company, takes reports, reads the announcements and orders for the day, then he calls the company to attention. Then he orders, "Everyone who has a mother take one step forward—not so fast there, Evans!"

I remember sitting on a table in the emergency room looking at my hand, which at that time was about the size, shape, and color of a football. I was on my third year clean and sober, yet I still handled anger by punching walls and doors. Of course, over the years of my using, all of the punched-out drywall and hollow-core doors in my home had been replaced through attrition. The doors were now solid birch and the walls were three-quarter-inch-thick pine. Did you ever try to punch through an inch-and-a-half-thick slab of laminated hardwood?

The doctor was filling out a form and she asked me, "How old are you, Barry?"

I blushed and said, "About ten."

It all has to do with someone I shared with at the meeting that night. He asked me, "What's the difference between addicts and savings bonds?"

I shook my head. "I don't know. What's the difference between addicts and savings bonds?"

"Bonds mature."

—◆—

The recovering mature, too, but change is slow as well as uneven and by degrees. One sponsee was telling his sponsor, "I'm stuck. I've been in the program for almost two years now, and I still feel terrible about myself."

His sponsor nodded and said, "You're making progress, though. When you first came into the program you had no self-esteem at all, right?"

"That's right."

"Now you have low self-esteem. That's progress."

—◆—

Another sponsor said to his sponsee, who he called The Walking Resentment, "You'll go far in this program."

The sponsee frowned even more deeply and asked, "What makes you say that?"

"You have so far to go."

130. Higher Powers and Old Business

At a Twelve Step convention meeting held very early in the morning, I heard something that splashed me wide-awake: "You don't have to damn the god of your childhood to acquire a higher power that will help you to recover. You don't have to damn him, but eventually you do need to forgive him."

After the meeting I shook my head in astonishment at my blind spots. Everyone and everything that has not been forgiven rests in my mind as a resentment, and resentments lead to relapse. Yet of all the persons and things that I had forgiven, the god of my childhood had been forgotten.

My intellectual too-smart-to-get-well self had rationalized away the whole issue. This god, who let me down at every turn, this god who was reputedly worshipped by those who injured me the most, this god who never listened and never spoke, obviously did not exist and never did. Hence, there was no need to forgive it. Perhaps the god hadn't been there, but the resentment was still alive and well.

That particular conference was held in early autumn at a Catholic monastery which makes a regular practice of hosting retreats and conventions held by various groups. It is a beautiful place set in the hills of rural southern Maine. Among the roads and trails that can be walked is a path lined with ancient oaks and maples, with fieldstone walls touched with moss and lichen. The path leads to a cemetery where the deceased brothers are buried, and beyond that is another cemetery for the Shakers who originally occupied the site.

It was on this path twelve years earlier that I had made a deal with my current higher power. The deal was, if I was still clean next year at this time, I would return. I've returned to that path every year since. Past the cemeteries and into the woods, the path forks. At the fork is a shrine to Jesus. Over the previous twelve years I had pretty much avoided the shrine. My entire experience with Jesus, his story, and his current followers made up out of TV evangelists, can-shakers, door-knocking missionaries, and sidewalk screamers left me with a super resentment hidden beneath an ocean of angry jokes.

The resentment was there, and the words of sponsors past told me, either you'll change, or you'll get high. There is only one payoff for hanging onto a resentment, and I don't want to go back. Anyway, it was time. I went to that shrine and stood there looking at a statue of a standing Jesus. There was a lot of blame for what happened to me that I associated with Jesus, and I could feel that letting go of this resentment would begin a considerable process of change.

Those voices again. "There is no healing until you run out of people to blame." I've known for a long time how to forgive. The program taught me to pray for the one I want to forgive.

I faced this statue and said, "I know that you are not responsible for the actions of those who invoke you or use your name. You are not my higher power, but you help a lot of my program brothers and sisters. Thank you for your life and your work." Then, to my higher power, I prayed for the best for Jesus.

131. A Peek at the Promise

Three and a half years before I went into rehab, I was put in an intensive care unit with a heart attack that had been going on for four days. It was my thirty-sixth birthday. The nurses shucked me naked and began sticking me full of pipes and needles as a technician stood off to one side ominously holding the paddles to a defibrillator. I said to the assembled company, "Is this a routine you people go through to keep out the riffraff?"

"Yeah," answered a male nurse with a grin. "It works, too."

Once I was hooked up, gowned, and covered, things seemed to calm down for a moment. I was propped up so that a portable X-ray unit could take a picture of my chest. When that was done, I was left sitting up so that I could talk to my wife and those in the room. That was when I felt my heart stop and all of the blood drain from my head. As I blacked out my last words were, "You better put me down."

Then I fell through the floor of the world into an infinite field of warm, black cotton. Everything I had ever been troubled about suddenly fell away, and I felt completely free and whole for the first time in my life. I was the same person—I was still me—but I was different: larger, complete. After a moment my consciousness seemed to expand until it encompassed everything and everyone in the world, then the galaxy, then the universe. I was filled with knowledge. I had no more questions. I knew everything, understood it all, and was at peace with it and myself. Everything in the universe happens for a reason and I knew what all of the reasons were. I could think of nothing but the thrill of spending the rest of eternity experiencing and exploring this phenomenal plane of existence.

I have heard of near-death experiences where the ones who encountered it approached a light through a tunnel and were offered a choice between going back to life or moving up the spiritual ladder. There was no tunnel and no light for me, and I don't think I was given a choice between staying and going back to the land of the living. Had the choice been mine, I would have stayed.

My life on earth then was a ruin, my relationships were in shambles, and every day was a desperate search to escape the physical and emotional pain of addiction. Next to that kind of life, my field of warm black cotton with its expansive knowledge and peace was so very attractive. The choice, however, appears to have been made for me.

At some point I found myself up in the corner of the ICU room looking down at my own body. Somehow neither my form nor the persons working frantically around my form seemed to have anything to do with me. I, who knew all and understood all, was coming back to life, which was something I could not accept. I had touched the infinite, had become a part of it, and then became whole. When I awakened inside my own body and felt the incredible peace, insight, and knowledge I had grasped so tightly dribble through my fingers until I was again my old self, I wept.

I entered the hospital addicted to alcohol. I left addicted to that and Valium, as well. Until I entered rehab, my near-death experience only visited me when I was feeling suicidal. The attraction of the place I had been was overwhelming. Equally overwhelming, however, was the single piece of knowledge that I managed to bring back with me: life is an incredibly valuable gift, not to be squandered away in a fit of rage or despair. From what I saw, there is no Heaven or Hell as such things are regarded. If I killed myself, though, I knew that I would join all of those who had betrayed me during my life: I would have betrayed myself; gypped myself out of knowing recovery; out of being, at last, a human. My business wasn't finished, which is why I was returned. Perhaps on some level I did choose to come back.

There is a universe of miracles waiting for each and every one of us. Most of us do not see the miracles because we are thoroughly focused on old injuries, current disappointments, and worries about the future. The Twelve Steps of recovery is a program designed to clear all of the old garbage from our heads and hearts, enabling us to see, experience, and enjoy the miracles that surround us and which we become in recovery.

There was a person in a meeting who was sharing about suicidal feelings. Afterward, an old-timer shared about his early recovery suicidal feelings. "And then I was told it would be a shame to kill myself the day before all the good things happen."

Today I know the miracle is there. Hang in there until you can see it, too.

132. The Write Stuff

Okay.

I am *bullshit!*

There I was, listening to the radio, happily doing the index for this book, when someone on the radio said something outrageously stupid. Very well, it's talk radio, and a talk radio shrink, at that. People call up with a problem and this one chugs out an answer after a few questions, and I don't like the radio shrink much. It is noise, however, and it does entertain somewhat the nine-tenths of my brain that has nothing to do during the indexing process.

So a man calls up. Seems he's about to celebrate his twenty-fifth anniversary in recovery, and his wife is planning a party at home with his family and a few friends. He has two children, seven and fourteen, and they don't know he's in recovery. They were never told why Daddy goes to those meetings, his wife thinks they ought to tell the kids what the celebration is all about, and now he wants to know if he should tell the kids.

My ears are all perked up, and the shrink begins giving the alkie some support noises about what a life lesson he is, and how you can get on the wrong track, and how difficult it is to turn your life around, and yabba, yabba, yabba.

Then the man says that the reason he hasn't told the kids is because it's a disease and—

And then the shrink comes down on him like stink in a shit storm. "A *disease*! If you're going to talk like that, I'm not going to talk to you anymore!" and then she hung up on the guy.

It seems that, despite all of the things I was taught in treatment, addiction is *not* a disease. Instead, it's a learned behavior that can be turned around by taking responsibility and control of your own life, and yabba, yabba, yabba.

The things I said to my radio. My, my, my.

My dog objected to one of the terms I was using. That was when I remembered another talk show host who also believes addiction is not a disease. This character, who could use about three Twelve Step programs I can think of (although I wouldn't want to take his inventory), believes addiction is a matter of choice. And I have to admit the term I called him was a slur on the names of billions of very useful sphincter muscles across the face of the planet.

In the 1950s, the American Medical Association officially recognized alcoholism as a disease, paving the way for addiction as a whole to be treated as a disease. It has a definable onset and a predictable outcome, meaning that it follows a characteristic course with known physical, psychological, and social symptoms. The disease can be arrested, not by "taking control of your life," but by turning control of your life over to a power greater than yourself and working a program of recovery.

And choice? I have yet to hear anyone say, "You know, what I want to be when I grow up is an addict. I've seen the recruiting posters and a life of puking all over my shoes and wetting my pants until my liver falls out looks exciting. Hell, I signed right up!"

Well, isn't there a point, before that first mood-altering substance, where you choose to take the risk of becoming addicted? Well, I became addicted in the womb. My mother, the addict, was doing coke and morphine the whole time she was carrying me. Just where was my choice?

What about that flight attendant I met on a return visit to rehab? She never used anything; then she got appendicitis. The surgeon who did the appendectomy screwed it up, she got a terrible infection, and during the subsequent treatment, she was given drugs for her pain. She became hooked, and once on the street, she was after anything she could get her hands on. From when her doctor first prescribed the pain killers until when the airline pulled an intervention on her, the flight attendant's entire using history lasted a little more than six months. Where was her choice? And millions of kids who are given sips of champagne on New Year's, and sips of beer, mama's pain killers, and hits off Uncle Charley's joint during the rest of the year by trusted parents and adults, where was their choice?

Okay, it's a disease. I know it's a disease. No one else but me needs to know that for my recovery. Everyone has a higher power, so I don't need to protect any newcomers or active users from those two talk show hosts. And since they believe exactly the same as I believed back when I was using, I can put this all to rest by stopping all this judgmental blustering, and doing what I have to do to forgive them. After all, most persons experienced in this disease and its treatment only get that way by getting the disease and getting into recovery.

Peace.

The above is an example of "writing it out," also called "finger puke." Writing is a program tool useful in taking the insane and rendering it sane. I don't usually publish my digit barf, but the insanity was there, the word processor was on, this document was up, and I thought an example might make a good meditation.

Why should you use writing in your recovery? There was a sponsee who once asked his sponsor, "Why should I write down my feelings and resentments?"

His sponsor answered, "It's so you can take the stuff in your head and put it on the paper, thereby making room for new information—and you are in serious need of new information."

133. In Nothing We Trust

If every time you came near a particular dog you hit it or kicked it, chances are if you reached out a hand to lovingly pet it, Fido is either going to cower in fear or sink his teeth into your hand. Humans are no different. If every time you trusted in someone you were hurt, let down, or betrayed, your ability to trust anyone would become impaired. This describes most of us who wind up in Twelve Step programs. This leaves us in a real pinch. To recover, one of the most important things we must do is do a lot of trusting: the program, a sponsor, meetings, anonymity, our fellow recoverers, and a higher power. The pinch is that we generally consider anyone who trusts anything either brain-dead or an idiot.

Experience forms how we see things. How we see things dictates how we feel about them. Trust is a feeling, and is, therefore, automatic. Our experience is that trusting anything is a good way to get slammed. What we do instead of trust, then, is mistrust. If we have to trust in order to recover, then how do we do that? If you want to change how you feel, you need to change how you see things. To change how you see things, you need to change your experience. In other words, to learn to trust you need to try it out.

My first experience in trusting happened on my first night in rehab. I couldn't sleep. I got some coffee, went to the patient lounge, and sat in the dark sipping the coffee, smoking my pipe, and mentally preparing my argument for what to say to my wife when I walked out of treatment and went back home to Maine the next morning.

As I ground my gears, another nighthawk came into the lounge carrying a coffee cup. There were at least forty empty places on the couches and chairs in the lounge, but he headed straight for me, sat next to me on the couch, and started talking.

In my head now we are all human, but back then my addiction made me ignorant and intolerant of other races, religions, and circumstances. He was a minister, and I didn't trust clergybeings of any stripe or description. He was a heroin addict, which to me meant he was a *real* drug addict, rather than a boozer and apprentice pill-popper like myself; and I didn't trust drug addicts. My experience with my family made me particularly mistrustful of the reality-challenged. Looking back, it's clear to me that my own reality was challenged.

He continued talking, though, about his life, the dreams he once had, his family and ministry, and how he had turned it all to shit with addiction. His pain was obvious, and he was telling me some awfully personal stuff. Then the light went on in my head: *this guy trusts me!*

He trusted me, he needed someone to talk to, and as he talked he seemed to relax and feel better. I considered his trusting me the most valuable gift I had been given in a very long time. That meant that at least this guy considered me trustworthy. I made up my mind right there never to betray a trust. And then I found my own mouth opening. I talked. I talked about my life, my dreams, my family and work, and how I had turned it all to shit with addiction. We were both crying and another light went on in my head: *I trust this guy*! My experience changed, how I saw things changed, and I made that first tentative move toward trust and recovery.

—◆—

"I can't trust anyone or anything," said a sponsee to her sponsor.

"If you don't change you are going to go back to the nightmare," said her sponsor. "That's the only payoff for not trusting, and that *is* something you can trust."

134. Attracting Promotion or Promoting Attraction

Well, the Eleventh Tradition says, "Our public relations policy is based on attraction rather than promotion; we need always maintain personal anonymity at the level of press, radio, and films." As was discussed in "There Is Death in a Name," there are good reasons for this, but I've seen world service–produced TV ads for AA, Al-Anon, NA, and Nar-Anon. It's hard not calling that promotion. Yet there is an NA convention whose current administration refuses to allow the NA logo on its T-shirts because of personal anonymity reasons.

It was not always like this. When this convention first started up, the T-shirts had the NA logo on them in big, bold letters surrounded by the name of the convention. And therein lies a tale.

My wife and I were in the United concourse at Chicago-O'Hare International Airport waiting for a connecting flight back from a science-fiction convention in California. I was wearing one of the old NA T-shirts and we were talking about the movie star we had met on the first leg of our flight. The entertainer had asked me what my T-shirt was all about. How to explain? I said, "It's a Narcotics Anonymous convention in Maine. It's a bunch of recovering drug addicts who meet every year to count noses to see who's still alive." Then he had wished us all good luck.

At our gate in Chicago, after my wife and I exhausted the movie star experience, I was getting out a book to read, when a young woman dressed in a food vendor uniform came up to me. "Hi," she said. "I've been clean for fourteen days, everybody I work with smokes dope, I'm going out of my mind, and I saw your T-shirt." The young woman, my wife, and I had an immediate hugfest and held an impromptu meeting right there. There was sharing, heads got screwed on straight, and when her break was over, the meeting ended.

So back to the Eleventh Tradition. Is it promotion? Attraction? I don't know. I wore an NA T-shirt, got a pat on the back from a movie star and got to help a fellow recovering addict through a rough afternoon. I'm keeping the T-shirt.

135. In Other Words . . .

Many of us are less than direct in expressing our needs or feelings. Many more of us are downright dishonest about it. Mix this with a bit of humor and all of the passive-aggressive personality skills we bring into the program, and the result is a collection of sayings that sound or look like one thing and mean something else.

For example, when someone in certain Twelve Step meetings is spouting off a full array of sickness, rationalization, and four-alarm craziness, the response he or she will get from the meeting is, "Keep coming back." This phrase, therefore, has come to mean: "You are really demented." There is an equivalent code phrase used by therapists. When they want to say, "You are full of shit," they say, "Thank you for sharing that."

The first time I realized that there is a meaning-slippage problem in the recovering, sometimes called "a vowel movement," was when a person in the program I dearly loved suddenly got it into her head that for some reason I was no longer trustworthy. That she felt this way was hurtful enough, but she took the opportunity to phone me several times to repeat her feelings without ever telling me what I was supposed to have done. On top of that, she phoned others in the program and told them, too!

Hurt, anger, more hurt, frustration, loss, and one big fat resentment. She began camping out in my head, and after a few weeks, I got tired of it. At the next opportunity I went way out of town and attended a meeting where I was sure that no one knew the object of my resentment. There I shared, talked it out, and made very good sounds about acceptance, forgiveness, detachment, and such.

After the meeting, a man came up to me and asked, "If you telephoned the woman you talked about, what would you really like to say to her?"

I thought about it, wrestled a few feelings, sent out a search for the program-appropriate response, and said, "I'd like to tell her that I forgive her . . . and *kiss my ass!*"

That was when I learned that the program meaning for "appropriate" is "lie," and that "I forgive you" . . . well, you get the drift.

The word "fine" has its own program spin. Its usual meaning is, "I don't want to talk about it," as in, "How are you doing?"

"Fine."

It is because of this that the honesty police in the program made "fine" into an acronym: FINE (Feeling Insecure, Neurotic, and Emotional. There are filthier versions.).

Some of the code responses take some imagination and effort to figure out. A sponsor asked her sponsee if she was getting any exercise. Responded the sponsee: "I'm into aerobic visualization."

After one meeting, I saw someone trying to thirteen-step a newcomer, who responded to the wannabe Don Juan, "Go lie with thyself and be fruitful."

One time I heard a blue flamer telling an old-timer what the old-timer was doing wrong in running his program. When the flamer finally concluded his rather insulting observations, the old-timer said, "Please take an aerial osculation at my gluteus maximus."

My favorite was one I had to look up myself. An elderly newcomer had just finished sharing about the lousy day he had been through. Absolutely nothing had gone right, except that he had not used and had made it to a meeting. A self-appointed meeting therapist asked, "Would you like some feedback?"

The newcomer glowered for a moment, and then said, *"Age, fac ut gaudeam."* It was some time later I learned that the phrase was Henry Beard's Latin translation of Dirty Harry's famous line, "Go ahead, make my day."

136. You Gotta Have Something

When I stumbled into rehab, the only drugs I knew about were alcohol, Librium, Valium, and Ativan, and I didn't call them drugs. Alcohol was a beverage and the rest were medicines prescribed for me by educated, well-meaning medical professionals who didn't know squat about either addicts or addiction. Drugs to me were those illegal street herbs and potions that I heard about on the news every time someone was running for reelection. In rehab talking to my fellow inmates, however, my drug education soared.

I learned about more ways and means to fry out a human brain than I can possibly list here. Back home in the program I learned about even more weeds, formulas, animal tranquilizers, and rat poisons. They were enough to cause my head to play with itself.

I mean, I managed to make it through the entire decades of the sixties and seventies without even trying marijuana. I never got into trouble with the stuff. Maybe I could use it safely. You gotta have something, right? And what about cocaine? I never tried that. Perhaps . . .

Those were scary days, sitting in the program meetings, toying with thoughts of trying out other drugs. At the time, I was only doing AA; NA was just getting started in Maine, and we had none of those meetings in our area. There were several alcoholics I knew who were doing marijuana maintenance, and there were others who were seeking a closer contact with their higher powers through prayer and medication. They didn't seem to last very long, but the principle remained. You gotta have something.

After we began our first NA meeting in my area, I learned about even more drugs, but I also had my nose rubbed in NA's description of itself: "This is a program of complete abstinence from all drugs."

That sounded needlessly inclusive to me, and my dragon did manage to focus my attention on the few members who considered alcohol or prescription mood-altering drugs something different from "drugs." As one beer drinker said to me, "My drug is heroin. I have a few beers once in a while and it's nothing. Hell, you gotta have something." It was curious how, on the one hand, his beer drinking was nothing, yet the excuse for it was "you gotta have something." What's even more curious is that I didn't pick up on that when he said it. Actually, when he said it, it made perfect sense to me. In other words, I was a wreck going someplace to happen.

The issue was clarified one night when, at our NA meeting, a newcomer was speaking and was describing how he felt the first time he tried cocaine. He was quite articulate, and had a genuine gift for description. He went off into a verbal euphoria about being filled with energy, enthusiasm, confidence, hope, and yea, even glory! As I listened, perched on the edge of my chair, my dragon's ears perked up, he jabbed me in the lobes and said, "Barry, that's *exactly what we were looking for!*"

My reaction was terror. I sat back in my chair, let out a breath that I had been holding for the previous five minutes, and said to myself, "Holy shit! I got addicted to cocaine just from hearing about it!" I decided then that cocaine and all other mood-altering drugs were not part of my program of recovery. Shortly after that I went through my own little nightmare of trying to stop smoking tobacco. A year later I tried it again, using the program, and it worked. Well, the program works on crack and heroin; why wouldn't it work on nicotine?

It was some years after that I came to a meeting a little early, and in one of the chairs sat a young newcomer who had about three months into the program. She was a very angry person who was also doing two other Twelve Step fellowships. Her big resentment was that she was just short of her twenty-first birthday. In another month it would be legal for her to drink. She was doing something that astonished me: puffing on a cigarette and coughing so hard I could almost see her lungs curl out of her mouth. I had never seen her smoke before.

"What are you doing?" I asked. "You don't smoke."

She finished coughing, shrugged, and said, "You gotta have something, and I don't believe that anyone can get addicted to these things."

— ◆ —

True, you gotta have something. Everyone who comes into a Twelve Step program makes it through the door with a universe-sized emptiness. We have spent lifetimes trying to fill that emptiness with substances and compulsive behaviors, and nothing was ever enough. We continue to look, though, and if we remain in the program long enough and work the Steps with enough diligence, we're going to find that "something" that we gotta have. Some say that this emptiness is a higher power sized hole to be filled in with the Eleventh Step. Regardless, the hole fills in as we grow in the program and heal physically, mentally, and spiritually. When I am tempted to take a shortcut and try to fill in that hole with something other than growth, I remind myself that the destination I would arrive at by going that particular route is not where I want to be.

137. Freebies

There is no program of abstinence from a compulsive behavior that doesn't have its apparent freebies—times when it appears necessary to engage in dangerous behavior. It is a rare recovering addict who, sooner or later, doesn't wind up in a doctor's office or in a hospital being offered "something for the pain." Overeaters have to eat, don't they, and now the medical community is telling us all that two alcoholic drinks a day is good for us. Mood-altering drugs and the recovering alcoholic/addict present a particularly threatening set of issues. Do I take it? What if I get hooked again? Are there any alternatives?

I had to go into the hospital for a rather stress-inducing procedure in which the cardiologist pops a hole in my groin and runs a pipe up my femoral artery into my heart for the purpose of squirting some stuff into my heart that makes one's pump show up on the little TV show they put on in there for the patient's entertainment. In preparation for this procedure, they usually prescribe a Valium to calm the patient. Before I could spend a second agonizing over whether to take or not to take the pill, someone near and dear to me told the doctor, the nurses and technicians, and everyone within a ten-mile radius that I was to have no mood-altering drugs.

Having this decision taken out of my hands bothered me somewhat, but I am a student of science and decided to make the best of things by taking an interest in the incredible technology involved. I don't know how long the procedure lasted. It seemed like no more than a few months. I watched my heart beating on the TV monitor for about nine seconds, then asked for the remote to do some channel surfing. I must have sweated out twenty pounds and wrung to death the hand that this one nurse let me hold while the fun and games were going on. I was so tense my lower back was one mass of screaming pain. What was even better, the next day I got to do the whole thing over again, this time with electrical wires in my heart zapping me in various tempos and combinations and making my heart jump around like a frog leg in a Daffy Duck biology experiment. I still get flashbacks from the experience that make me shudder.

Two years later, I got to do the electrical variation one more time. In the intervening period, someone near and dear and I had had a talk about hospital medications and whose decision it is whether to go for the pill. As it happened, I took the Valium, went through the procedure calmly, and that was that. I was slightly disappointed that I didn't get a buzz, but once out of the hospital I did a meeting.

Mood-altering drugs for medical reasons. I have seen recovering addicts go for them, refuse them, and catch hell both ways. There are program officers who insist that any use of mood-altering drugs, no matter what the medical reasons are, constitute a relapse. None of these purists have had limbs amputated or have cancer. Then there are the program hippies who figure, hey, if the doctor says to take it, go for it. These guys could have a foot amputated and they wouldn't notice, save for the tilt.

Over the years, this issue has come up for me and others many times. Our experience has led us to a few conclusions. First, be completely honest with your doctor. Tell the doctor that you are a recovering addict, and will be at risk taking mood-altering drugs. Second, take it for granted that your doctor hasn't a clue what this means. Remember, your recovery is *your* responsibility, not the doctor's.

Third, take pain killers, relaxants, or other mood-altering drugs only under supervision. If in a hospital, make certain they detox you before discharging you. If you have a prescription you have to take at home, either dump the pills down the toilet or give them to a friend to administer to you according to the prescription. If the doctor has overprescribed, have the friend toss them down the toilet *before* you think you don't need them anymore. Also, stay close to the program and your sponsor, and work your program like canoeing in a flood: paddle like there is no god and pray like you have no paddle.

Take this seriously. After hearing these suggestions, a person with a couple of years in the program said that it wasn't necessary to make a warden out of a friend to hand out medications. That kind of stuff was overdoing it. Her eventual undoing was a prescription cough medicine that contained codeine. Within three months she was back out, back into her chosen drug, and was dead of an overdose. She is only one of many examples.

There is no need to put yourself through unnecessary physical pain from a medical condition, but listen when your sponsor says that you might be using a medical condition to work the medical community for pops and drops. As one old-timer put it, "To an addict, there ain't no such thing as a freebie."

138. Happy Humbugs

Three addicts die and go to Heaven. Outside the Pearly Gates, St. Peter faces them and says, "Before I can let you through, we have a little test you must take." He faces the first addict and asks, "Can you tell me what Easter is?"

The addict frowns, searches through his remaining memories, and says, "Easter. Isn't that when you sit in the pumpkin patch and wait for the Great Pumpkin to appear and give gifts to all the boys and girls?"

St. Peter stares at the person for a moment, then he looks at the second addict. "What is Easter?" he asks.

The second addict scratches his head and says, "Isn't Easter the one where you set off a lot of fireworks and then go eat a turkey with cranberry sauce?"

St. Peter sighs and looks at the third addict. "Can you tell me what Easter is?"

The third addict nods and says, "Two thousand years ago in the land of Galilee there was a great teacher who taught that we should love one another. He performed many miracles. His teaching offended those in power, and he was tried and crucified. His body was placed in a tomb and a great stone was rolled in front of the entrance, sealing it. On the third day he rose from the dead, rolled the stone away from the tomb's entrance, stepped out in the light, saw his own shadow, went back into his tomb and there were six more weeks of winter."

— ◆ —

A large number of us have problems with holidays. While everyone around us is wishing one another "Happy [insert holiday here]!," and "Happy New Year," many of us are muttering, "Bah, humbug!" and approaching holidays with everything from indifference and hatred to gloom and suicidal despair. We all know the reasons. Many of us come from affected homes where holidays were occasions for drinking, using, and causing a great deal of pain. For others, holidays were times to compare the families in which we found ourselves to the seemingly happy families of our schoolmates or those illusions of families on television.

For many of us, the pain goes much deeper. The biggest holidays seem to be centered around gods or other figures and institutions of authority, all of which let us down, failed to protect us, and in some cases actively joined in the process of creating for us a hell on earth.

Mother's Day is often an occasion for pain and bitterness, both for mothers and those of us who once had mothers who were less than adequate. As we were approaching Mother's Day one time, there was a woman at a meeting in a great deal of pain. She was sharing about how her son in active addiction used to abuse her, and now ignores her every single Mother's Day, although he never fails to call if he needs a baby-sitter, some money, or something else. At the meeting we decided that mothers in the program who don't get remembrance cards from their screwed-up children should be, instead, sent a card by their mothers that reads:

> *Roses are red,*
> *Violets are blue,*
> *I may be a mother,*
> *But so are you.*

Comparing our holiday experiences with what we think they should have been is dragon chow: a setup for unhappiness and eventual failure. Using holidays to polish up old hurts, resentments, and bitterness fattens up the dragon, because the dragon knows if it can make remaining abstinent more painful than using, you'll use. But what to do about holiday blues? In general, do the same thing the program suggests doing with spirituality. Make them holidays *of your understanding.*

With Christmas, for example, I celebrate Mithras and Nicholas. December 25th was the officially recognized birthday of Mithras long before the Christians borrowed the date, the holiday, and the illuminated tree; and I always did like Santa Claus. With New Year's, I officially put the old year to rest and renew my positive outlook for what's coming up as long as I continue to grow in recovery. Valentine's day? I have a lot of folks I love nowadays, and I try and let them know. On St. Patrick's Day I make amends to a snake, and on Palm Sunday, I wash mine.

The point is: look for something to celebrate, keep your focus there, and *celebrate*. I learned how to do this from the British, who have a holiday called Guy Fawkes Day. Mr. Fawkes tried to blow up King James I and Parliament in an exercise known as the Gunpowder Plot, November 5, 1605. Officially, the holiday celebrates the foiling of the plot and the preservation of both monarch and Parliament. I have found celebrants, however, who use the occasion to honor the conspirators and their bold attempt to clean house, as it were. Because the holiday usually falls around Election Day in the United States, I have taken to celebrating Guy Fawkes Day myself. I celebrate either the foiling of the plot or the attempt to level the place, depending on where I am with this problem I have with authority.

Choose a happy holiday.

139. Say Three Good Things about Yourself

Step Four says, "We made a searching and fearless moral inventory of ourselves." Nowhere does it say "We proceeded to kick the snot out of ourselves," but that is what many of us make out of the Fourth. It's supposed to be an inventory of assets as well as liabilities, but very few of us who make it into Twelve Step programs can accept that we might have any assets at all. That takes work.

In rehab, I was going through what passed for Fourth Step preparation when, in group, my counselor interrupted my self-deprecating humorous monologue by saying, "Barry, I want you to say three good things about yourself."

And there I was, caught between people-pleasing and low self-esteem. This particular counselor wasn't about to let me get away with a blush, holding my hands behind me, giving her an "Aw, shucks," and drawing circles on the floor with my toe, but that was all I could think of. I felt like a cornered rat. I was desperate. Three good things about myself. Impossible.

It goes like this: the dragon wants me to use. The more miserable I am, the more likely it is that I will use. The unhappier I am about myself, the more miserable I will be. The more evil I consider myself, the unhappier about myself I will be. I had spent my life up until then working that misery machine. And this character wanted me to say *three good things about myself*!

I never said good things about myself. My style was to fish for compliments and then regard the compliments as insincere when I would get them. Then I remembered one of many Thanksgivings from hell and from where I got my style.

The family was seated at the dining room table and, after having cooked for endless hours, my mother stood there barefooted in her flannel night-gown, her hair going every which way, fishing for compliments. "Is the dinner all right? I thought the turkey might be a little dry."

Where do intelligence and good sense go when they flee? My father, already well into his second double Martini, said, "Yes. I believe you're right. It is a little dry."

Of course, he was drunk. He had an excuse. Like a herd of lemmings, though, the rest of us followed with our confirmations. Yes indeedy, the bird was definitely a tad on the parched side. The ensuing blast from my mother singed eyebrows throughout a five-county area and permanently changed weather patterns in the northern hemisphere. Every holi-day after that, she could have served up a saddlebag stuffed with old sneakers and when asked if it were a bit on the dry side, we would protest and bear wit-ness to the perfection of the feast as we rolled our eyes, rubbed our tummies, and went into spasms of lip-smacking ecstasy.

That's what I was afraid of: saying something good about myself and having someone in the group say, "That's a load of crap. You aren't that."

I did finally come up with three things. They weren't things I believed, but they were things I could document in case anyone wanted to argue with me. For example, I said that I was a good writer, although I was convinced I was a fraud. I had several books out, though, as well as a number of awards. I could back up my claims by reaching outside of myself. There was nothing inside of me, however, that agreed.

Six months later, in a growth group in Maine, a young woman fresh from rehab shared something that made me realize that I hadn't changed. She said that her counselor had asked her to say five good things about herself.

"*Five* things!" I thought to myself, half in shock at the horror of the chore as I flashed back to my own three good things experience. "What a burden!"

Later that night while driving home, I thought about the three good things I said about myself in rehab. They were bullshit. They were true, but bullshit all the same. I hadn't said anything good about myself that *I believed*. I asked myself, "Is there nothing good about me that I do believe?" The road was very dark and lonely and I was full of despair about my chances of recovery, when from inside of me I heard, "I have been clean and sober for six months."

It was something that only I knew for certain. There was no way I could prove it to anyone, yet I believed it, and felt very good about it. It was something I could and did say to others without fear of being "found out." As I thought about that, I could physically feel something inside of me turn around. Before I reached home I found other things that were good about me, things I now had the ability to see and believe: courage, caring, compassion, kindness, a sense of humor—

I couldn't prove any of it. What's more important, I didn't need to.

Then I remembered the story about Francis of Assisi and his garden. Someone commented to the monk that his garden was very beautiful and that he must have prayed a lot.

Francis answered, "True, but every time I prayed I picked up a hoe."

Rehab, growth group, meetings, working the Steps—I had put in a great deal of hard work to achieve this change in how I look at myself, which gave me another unprovable good thing I could say about myself and that I believe: I work hard. Of course, one of the things I have to work hard at is abstaining from workaholism.

Go ahead. Say three good things about yourself, and keep using all of the tools of recovery you can get your hands on until you can believe the three good things. Then try that Fourth Step. It's supposed to be an inventory, not an indictment.

Important safety tip: do your Fourth as though there is no Fifth Step. If you worry about reading your Fourth to your sponsor at the same time you're writing it, a magical editor will appear and begin editing your writing for publication, blue-penciling out the most important things. The price of this is an incomplete inventory; something less than "searching and fearless." That magical editor is the dragon, and it does have an agenda that is very unhealthy—for you.

If you have any sense at all, you will take your completed Fourth Step, make the proper arrangements, and do a Fifth Step as soon as possible. As with supermarket meat and produce inventories, moral inventories begin to stink when not used.

140. Sponsors from Hell

In all things, there are some of us who need extra. This is true with the very important relationship of having a sponsor. At one meeting an addict was sharing about an experience he had years before with his sponsor. "We were at a diner and I was telling him how much I wanted to die. Things were so awful, I just couldn't stand thinking about facing another hour alive. I wouldn't listen to any of this gratitude shit. I just wanted to die. My sponsor listened to all of it, then asked me to go outside. We went to his pickup truck, opened the door, and I watched as he pulled a handgun out from beneath the driver's seat.

"'I want to help you. How 'bout we go to a quiet place and take care of your problem?'

"I looked at that gun, shook my head, and squeaked, 'Nope.'

"'You don't want to die?'

"'Nope.'

"'Just having a bad day?'

"'Yup.'

"Then he put the gun away and we worked on starting my day over."

— ◆ —

At a speaker's meeting, the speaker was sharing about his sponsor who, as the speaker put it, did not believe in unconditional love. In the meeting where the speaker got clean and sober, they had a three-month rule: you had to have at least three months of sobriety before you were allowed to speak.

"I was champing at the bit to get up there and speak. I was brimming with brilliant things and inspiring messages to share with the others. Finally, my third month of sobriety behind me, the chairperson at the meeting called upon me to speak. I jumped up, ready to fill the hall with my intellect, when my sponsor grabbed me by the seat of my pants and pulled me back down. Then he said, in a very loud whisper, 'You go up there, tell 'em your name and that you're a drug addict and alcoholic, then sit down, 'cause that's all you know.'"

— ◆ —

Early in my own recovery, I went to my sponsor boxed in by gloom, deprivation, powerlessness, and self-pity. "I can't drink, I can't drug, I can't play cards, I can't eat like I want, I can't smoke, and now with this heart problem, I can't even use goddamned butter or real coffee!"

He shrugged and shook his head. "You're wrong. You can do all those things. C'mon, grab your coat. I bet I can score you any drug you want in less than fifteen minutes."

"Fifteen minutes?" I said, wondering if I had somehow stumbled on the world's craziest sponsor. I would've begun edging toward the door, but I was afraid he'd take that as consent to go on a drug hunt.

"Sure," he answered. "The only people in this town who don't know who and where the dealers are are the cops, and they're paid not to know."

"But I can't do drugs."

"Sure you can. You *choose not to do them.* When you can't do any of these things, you feel deprived. But the power is yours. You choose not to do those things because they aren't good for you."

The pressure on me, the sense of deprivation, lifted, although I was left with a nagging doubt. I asked my sponsor, "What if I had taken you up on going out and buying me some drugs. Would you?"

He smiled broadly and shook his head as he went to the door, reached into an umbrella stand, and pulled out a very large baseball bat. He grinned as he stood there smacking the business end of the bat against his palm. I almost have myself convinced that he was joking.

—◆—

There were identical twin brothers, Amal and Juan, who entered recovery and eventually became sponsors. One of Amal's sponsees went to Amal's house to talk to him, but Amal's wife, Debbie, said that her husband had to work late. Just then, however, Juan drove up, returning the lawn mower he had borrowed from his brother. Debbie said to the sponsee, "There's Juan. He's in recovery. You can talk to him."

"But I wanted to see Amal," protested the sponsee.

Debbie shrugged and said, "If you've seen Juan, you've seen Amal."

141. A Different Kind of Fifth

Step Five says, "We admitted to God, to ourselves, and to another human being the exact nature of our wrongs."

The Fifth Step is probably the easiest and most difficult Step in the dozen. It's easy because all you have to do is take that Fourth step, call in your higher power and yourself as observers, and read that Fourth out loud to your sponsor or someone else that you trust.

"I know everything that's in my Fourth Step," said a sponsee to his sponsor. "Why do I have to read this to you?"

The slightly sarcastic answer was, "It's hard to spot self-deception by yourself."

Doing a Fifth Step is difficult because, for the very first time in our lives, we become completely vulnerable. We let someone know the real us, bells, whistles, snakes, warts, and all. Once we do that, though, a miracle happens: we begin discovering that we are human.

142. The Friends We Left Behind

To recover, the program taught me that I would have to change my playthings, playgrounds, and playmates. One of the things that made recovery scary for me was giving up those intensely close friendships I used to have, like, for example, drinking with my very dear friends. I have never felt so close to another human being as I did one night at a science-fiction convention in Philadelphia. As usual, I was camped out where the free booze flowed, and I was sitting on a couch with a friend, who was also drinking. We were talking about very important stuff: meaningful, relevant, deep. I was having such an intellectual and emotional rapport with this fellow, I could not imagine how anything could blemish it. My friend then looked at me, vomited in my lap, and passed out, his face splashing in my lap as he collapsed. I looked down at my lap, saw my friend slumbering there, became thoroughly grossed out, and barfed on my companion's head.

I don't remember what we talked about, I don't remember my friend's name, nor even what he looked like without all of those gastronomic decorations. My friends today, I value much more. They are real, we know and remember each other, they are there for me when I need them, and there are fewer cleaning bills. Ah, the gifts of recovery.

—◆—

Remember, recovery is like a sewer. You only get out of it what you put into it. Be selective.

143. The Twelve Slips

1. I insisted I was in control and my life was quite manageable.
2. I came to believe only in what I could see, and regarded those who didn't believe the same as crazy.
3. I made a decision to write everybody out of my will, and told them all to go to the Devil.
4. I made a searching and fearless moral inventory of everyone else.
5. I assured myself, and all those who were nagging me, that I was perfect.
6. I was entirely ready to remove all these defective characters.
7. I angrily demanded that they get the hell out of my life.
8. I made a list of all those I resented and became willing to see every one of them rot in Hell.
9. I loudly demanded the amends that were due me.
10. I never wasted my time taking personal inventory because I was never wrong.
11. I sought through flair and medication to increase control over myself and others.

12. Having relapsed countless times, I kept telling everyone that I don't have any problems that can't be cured by everyone else in the world doing things *my way*!

144. Inside Outside

Alcoholics Anonymous has no opinion on outside issues; hence the A.A. name ought never be drawn into public controversy.
—Tradition Ten

The entire time I was in rehab, I don't think I read the Twelve Traditions all the way through even once. I was scrabbling for my life, so what did I care about public controversy? My only interest in public controversy was to get myself out of it. It was later that the need for Tradition Ten became very clear.

Some time ago, a couple of interesting propositions were introduced to the Twelve Step program's world service organization. The first one was to drop the word "God" from the Steps and Traditions. The second proposition was to make the Steps and Traditions gender-neutral. You just know that somewhere some well-meaning do-gooder decided to bring his or her Twelve Step program into the modern world. Sides were chosen, and the program membership has been unraveling ever since, with the sad result of driving away newcomers and old-timers alike.

Okay, so what is an "outside issue?" There are many gray areas: Is addiction a disease? Can an alcoholic return to social drinking through behavioral modification? Are rehab programs a help or a hindrance to recovery? Should drug possession and use be decriminalized?

Then there are issues where there is no doubt that they are "outside." Among these: Who should be prime minister of England? Should Quebec separate from the rest of Canada? Should the president of the United States wear boxers or briefs? Should Iceland host the next Summer Olympics?

There are, in addition, two more: In the English language, can the noun "man" and the pronoun "he" refer to both males and females? Is God's name "God?"

A sponsor once told me, "If you think a friendship or a business relationship is going too well, pick a political position and insist that the other guy agree with you." It seems that through the same means one can shatter a fellowship. A PC program officer of my acquaintance, however, held that the gender-neutral thing and dropping "God" from the Steps and Traditions are not outside issues. "We use these terms in our literature. What we do with them, then, is important to us and is only our business."

By the same token, though, many Twelve Step meetings take place in the basements of banks, churches, synagogues, and mosques. Perhaps we should take a position on which one of these institutions has the inside track? I mean, it's about the nature and meaning of existence. We and the programs exist. Isn't that important? We may have to wear body armor and carry assault rifles to meetings, but what the hell, it's "our business."

The term "God," however, offends some people. That's why the suggestion to remove it was made. Hell, when I was a newcomer, the term "sober" offended me. What really put the blood in my eye, though, was the word "normal." Nothing, however, pissed me off quite as much as the question, "You got a sponsor yet?"

Yes, when I was new in the program, the word, the sound, and the many concepts of "God" offended me, as did the term "higher power." For a long time in meetings I refused to say the Serenity Prayer, because of the word that starts the thing off. The first lesson I needed to learn from this was not to rewrite the literature; it was tolerance. Through tolerance, I learned that it is not "God," it is "God *as we understood him,*" which covers everything from Alexander the Great and St. George, through the inner self and the unconscious, to teddy bears, the Universe, and Mother Earth. I no longer object to the name "God." My occasional use of it to refer to the universe of which we are all parts I regard as a sign of tolerance acquired.

People adapt according to their lights. I have seen those who did not like the name "God" do meeting readings of the Steps by substituting "higher power" for the word "God." Those with another agenda substitute the word "God" for the male pronouns, as in,

"We made a decision to turn our will and our lives over to the care of God *as we understood God.*"

I have heard, as well, the term "Goddess" substituted, as well as "she" for all of the times "he" appears. These events were further opportunities for tolerance, and I have no objection to these terms, either. It shows me, though, what the net program effects of the above controversies will be, if the proposed changes are ever made. Those who want to use the name "God" will substitute it for whatever generic term is selected, and English traditionalists will substitute the pronoun "he" for he/she, or whatever the gender-neutral winner is. In other words, there will be no substantial changes, except for all of the current members and newcomers who will be driven away from recovery by all the bad feelings, which appears to incinerate Tradition Five: Each group has but one primary purpose—to carry the message to the [addict, alcoholic, etc.] who still suffers."

Actually, this all has more to do with Tradition One: "Our common welfare should come first; personal recovery depends upon [EIEIOA] unity."

Unity, folks.

With it we recover. Without it—well, you remember what it was like all alone, don't you?

145. Dirty Harry on Opinions

Speaking of controversies, it was during the notorious Anita Hill Senate hearings when my appointment with a periodontist for gum surgery came due. The masked medical banditos had me stretched out on the couch of pain when in came my doctor. He, too, was masked and gloved. In addition, he had on a set of earphones. I asked him about them and he responded that he was listening to the Anita Hill hearings on the radio. In addition, from his comments, I deduced that we were on different sides of the issue.

In my continuing program of growth within Twelve Step recovery, I had just been learning that failing to voice my opinions was part of my people-pleasing defect. I would keep silent while others voiced their opinions, listening and gleaning among the sentiments for something with which I could agree. Hence, everyone assumed I agreed with them and no one got angry or impatient with me. The new me, however, had opinions that were just as valid as anyone else's. I was learning that I matter, and my opinions matter, at least as much as anyone else's.

I was thinking of all this as the doctor, muttering beneath his breath as he urged on his side at the hearing, climbed into my mouth with a fistful of sucking hoses and a variety of razor-sharp implements. What about my side? What about integrity? What about defending my opinion? That's when I remembered Dirty Harry's famous observation, "Opinions are like assholes: everybody's got one." The program equivalent is: "How important is it?"

I let go of it, kept my mouth shut—figuratively speaking—and let the man with all the forks and knives do his work. After all, as that great radical bomb-maker back in the sixties, Shaky Gordon, once said, "Timing is everyth—"

146. How to Choose "No"

In rehab one night, I received a strange bit of feedback. Some of my group mates and I were sitting in our wing's patient lounge talking about boundaries and assertiveness. I was sharing that, as with most people-pleasers, I never learned how to set boundaries. I gave a couple of examples to show how hopeless I was, and then came the feedback. It was from a newcomer to the group who was, by trade, a sex worker. "You know, Barry, if you were in my line of work, you would be an absolute failure. You just can't say no." I wasn't sure whether to take that as a compliment or criticism. Hence, I took it for a criticism.

I remembered her comment many times after I returned home from treatment, especially when someone would call me on the telephone to ask me to do something. My career was just getting off its back, and, with a bit of notoriety, college, high school, and elementary school teachers across the region were asking me to come and talk to their classes about writing. When I would say, "Sure," I would hear this little squeal of delight from the caller, and that was my reward, which didn't quite cover the price: being angry with myself for weeks.

Time is my principal raw material. If I use it driving three hours each way to put on a two-hour entertainment for some teacher's students, I am not using it writing. Some of these events I enjoy, however, and I sometimes get to do some real good, which I also enjoy. I can't afford to spend all my time doing this, though, so how do I achieve some kind of balance? While I was thinking about that, the phone rang and a teacher at a school several hours away asked if I could come and talk to her students about writing.

I literally could not say no. After I agreed and hung up, I stared at the wall, so angry with myself that I was driven to ask my current higher power to enlighten me on what I should do about these phone requests. In less than a minute I wrote down the following:

How to Choose "No"
1. Say "I'll get back to you."
2. Hang up.
3. Pretend that the person who called you just dropped dead.
4. Ask myself, "Is this [request] something I really want to do?"
5. Answer the question.
6. Call the person back and give your decision.

The third step in this list is not a vengeance fantasy. Instead, pretending that the caller is dead removes the people-pleasing weight from the decision. I posted my list of steps next to the telephone, and it worked well for me until I grew to the point where I could make a decision about what I did or didn't want to do without either hanging up the phone or mentally killing anyone.

147. How to See the Bleeding Obvious

A guy says to his doctor, "Doctor, it hurts when I do that." The doctor says, "Don't do that."
—Henny Youngman

In rehab there was a poster on the wall of my counselor's office. It said, "An alcoholic is someone who takes one leaf and from it grows a forest in which he immediately becomes lost."

Keep it simple. This slogan is the bedrock upon which quality recovery is built. Everything else in the program, including the other slogans, are the results of putting in practice the principle of "Keep it simple." Yet how many times have I watched myself and others in the program get tangled in endless mental convolutions guaranteed to paralyze recovery, evaporate serenity, and open that door back to the nightmare?

At one stage of my adventure in recovery, I went to my sponsor with a problem. I was going to a total of six meetings a week, and I wore that fact like a medal that proclaimed I should be doing great. Yet I wasn't getting any better. I walked around in a constant state of apprehension and gloom, while serenity had become a bitter joke. Was I one of those for whom recovery is impossible?

"Before you go and do something uniquely stupid," began my sponsor, "tell me about the meetings you attend."

At the time I was going to one NA meeting, two AA meetings, one OA meeting, an Al-Anon meeting, and an ACA meeting. With further prompting, I revealed that I really loved the NA meeting, one of the AA meetings, and the OA meeting. The other AA meeting and the Adult Children of Alcoholics meeting were so lightly attended that I often found myself alone and always felt obligated to show up, because if I didn't show up there probably wouldn't be any meeting at all. At the Al-Anon meeting I felt very unwelcome, like I was the enemy, as though I should be wearing a bell and calling out to warn everyone, "Unclean! Unclean!"

My sponsor looked at me as though I had just asked him where my nose was, then he asked me, "Why are you doing that to yourself?"

"Doing what?" I asked, utterly baffled.

"There are three meetings you go to for recovery—the three meetings you like. Then there are two meetings you go to because of self-imposed obligations—guilt—and an additional meeting you attend because you must like feeling like shit. You've heard it before: Climb down off the cross; we need the wood."

I was getting help at three meetings and hurting myself with the other three meetings. That was when I remembered Henny Youngman's joke about "Doctor, it hurts when I do that." And the doctor answers, "Don't do that."

My wife freaked when I cut out the three meetings that were hurting me, since the usual first sign of an impending relapse is cutting down on meetings. The result, however, was relief; as though a thousand tons of obligation and disapproval had been lifted off me. It stayed off until, ten years later, I once again found myself doing my best to prop up three meetings that were going under and leaving a two-year-long trail of gloom, resentment, and despair wherever I went.

At one of these gatherings, a third of the meeting said, "We're doing our best to do everything right, yet we're dying and feeling miserable about it."

As I listened to her, like the spirits of ancient oracles, the voices from the past reached through the years and whispered in my ear:

> *"Doctor, it hurts when I do that."*
> *"Don't do that."*

Another thing occurred to me, as well. Trying to figure out what to do about it for myself was too much. If a sponsee of mine came to me with the same problem, though, the solution would be obvious. I'd tell him to drop the meetings he was going to because of self-imposed obligations and exchange them for meetings where he can go to get recovery. We made a pact that night to let go and go where the recovery lives. Curiously enough, we found it right where we had left it.

Keep it simple by keeping it simple.

148. When Is It Going to Get Better?

The program must be working; I feel like shit.
—Anonymous

When I first came into the program, I made a deal and it went like this: once I am in recovery, never again will I have any problems. In its own perverse way, however, life seemed to have waited until I was trying to stay clean and sober before dropping upon my head endless loads of crap. Each time problems would land on me, then, it seemed as though somebody or something had let me down. It took some time, experience, and some wiser heads to show me that the program never promised me I would never again have problems. Problems are a part of life. What I would get from the program are the tools I would need to deal with the problems that would arise.

This is how it has worked for me. I look back at the things I thought were problems back during my first year, and they are pale things indeed compared to the current selection. Yet today my load of problems seems much lighter than what I was carrying during my first year. The difference is in what I have learned in the program over the years about acceptance, letting go, setting boundaries, treating myself with respect, taking risks, and asking for help.

"But when is it going to get better?" demands a newcomer. The usual old-timer response is, "It always gets better. It doesn't always feel better, but it always gets better."

There is pain. Disappointment, conflict, and loss. Over time, and working the program, we learn how to deal with pain by going through it, rather than by trying to bury it with drugs, food, booze, or something else. We also learn that we are responsible for our actions, and that acts have consequences. By working with this, instead of ignoring it or fighting it, we learn how to quit setting ourselves up for disaster, with a net reduction in pain.

We learn that the meaning of life is life itself, and that the measure of success at its end is neither wealth nor fame nor power. The measure of success is love; our love of others, their love of us, our love of life and the adventure of living.

Put another way, recovery is not a goal, it is a process. There ain't no such thing as a "recovered" addict. Drinking problems don't just go away. There are things to do every day to be granted recovery for that day. Do the footwork and the rest will take care of itself. In my early attempts at trying out a higher power, one of the messages I got was to do my best—at recovery, at my work, at my life. Do my best, and my HP will do the rest. My best. That is what I consider my "duty," as in "Do your duty, always; but without attachment," from the *Bhagavad-Gita*. There was another way I heard it said. At a meeting an old-timer said, "Many make themselves miserable and miss recovery by waiting for it to happen. Recovery is not a destination; it is a journey. The joy is in the journey."

149. Fun with Time

The guy chairing the meeting was nine days older than God, and this was a meeting whose members were mostly college students. He began by saying his name followed by, "I know a lot more about being young than you know about being old, so listen up."

After his qualification, the meeting proceeded, and among the sharing that followed, there were several joking references to the chairperson's advanced years. A few of the references were downright cruel, and I was amazed at how all of this nasty ribbing seemed to sail right past him. He appeared to take absolutely nothing personally. In fact, throughout the entire meeting he seemed to be laughing at a secret joke.

After the meeting, gathered around the coffeepot, one of the nastier jokesters went up to the old guy and said, "None of this gets to you, does it, old man? You're ancient, you're cripping around on a cane, your hands shake, a bunch of us are giving you shots, and you laugh. Do you have a corner on forgiveness, a super Serenity Prayer in your pocket, or what?"

The old guy smiled and shook his head. "No, youngster. It's just that I know something you don't."

"What's that?"

The old guy pointed at himself. "You see this old wreck?"

"Yeah."

"If you are very, very lucky, young man, the exact same thing is going to happen to you. What's more, even if the years eat so many holes in your brain you can't remember your own name, you will remember some old guy you made fun of and who laughed at you for doing it. By then you'll have figured out why he was laughing."

150. It's My Party and I'll Slip If I Want To

Where do you go on New Year's Eve if you want to stay clean and sober? If you don't want to get blown away, don't party in a minefield. That's simple enough— I thought. A couple in recovery invited my wife and I to usher in the New Year at their place, and we eagerly accepted the invitation. It had been years since we'd gone out to a New Year's party. Even today I am uncomfortable around people who are using drugs, and alcohol is on the top of that list. Besides, how much enjoyment can you get out of some drunk boring you with the same story for the fifth time? A program-safe party was going to be some big fun.

After spiffing up and donning our riot threads, we arrived at the appointed time. The first thing to greet us was one of our recovery friends, the hostess. The second thing that greeted us were eight tons of high-test alcohol fumes: rum, gin, scotch, blended whiskey, vodka, and wines of various vintages and shades. All the guests we could see had drinks, and several were half in the bag. The feelings I had at the time gave a whole new meaning to the phrase "a fish out of water."

Our two program friends weren't drinking, and neither was their teenage son, also in the program. The son was serving as the bartender. I looked at my wife, she looked at me. I have seen confusion before, but the look on her face matched mine, I am certain. We played games with the situation for a while. After all, they were our friends, and it's an individual program; perhaps we were giving too much power to alcohol, how important is it, judge not lest ye be judged, and . . . we got the hell out of there! They say if you don't want to slip, stay away from slippery places, and that place was a buttered tube straight back to the nightmare.

Later, at a Twelve Step meeting, an old-timer shared that when he was new in the program, and for about three years thereafter, he kept a bottle of gin in his kitchen cabinet for guests, and to prove that the program had broken alcohol's power over him. "No guests ever asked for a drink," he said, "so the bottle just sat there, unopened, for all that time. I didn't drink, but I always knew that bottle was there. Finally, I figured out I don't have to prove anything to anyone and to hell with the guests. I threw out the gin and that's the day when my serenity began."

They told me in rehab that addiction is the disease that tells you that you haven't got it. It also provides the user with a very selective memory and a life-threatening set of priorities oriented around using. If it keeps us using, it's good. If it interferes with our using, it's bad. Once we stop using, those priorities don't automatically change. It takes a lot of work with the Twelve Steps and a lot of growing up before our choices begin to reflect those of a life-form with a sane sense of self-preservation.

This is why the following exchange took place at a meeting. A fellow was sharing about how he was going to throw a party and was planning on stocking up a good supply of booze for his drinking guests because—well, for most people, what's a party without alcohol, and "Drinking doesn't make me uncomfortable."

"Assume that it does make you uncomfortable," said an old-timer. "You'll live longer."

Another way of putting it is, the sickest one is the one who doesn't know how sick he is.

151. The Forgotten Relationship

The way it was put to me early in the program was, "To recover you are going to have to renegotiate every relationship in your life." When I heard that, I could see why I'd have to do that with my wife. By the time I made it into rehab, her main problem was trying to choose between divorce and homicide. The next relationships that made the necessity for renegotiation apparent were those with our two pet cats. They were both nervous cases, terrified of raised voices and sudden movements. After much peace, love, and patience, they forgave me and eventually wanted to be with me all the time, which was something else I needed to renegotiate with my wife, who considered the cats hers.

There was little to renegotiate with using friends. When I got clean and sober, they vanished. The renegotiation had to do with grieving, acceptance, and valuing myself enough not to pursue them by going back to the old nightmare. Then there were sisters and brothers. In some cases it was the same as with using friends, except that the grieving was longer, the acceptance harder, and valuing myself all the more difficult to justify.

Difficult relationships to renegotiate were my parents, both dead from addiction at the time of bargaining. Rage, anger, bitterness, and finally forgiveness and acceptance, all of which had to be negotiated all over again when I went through the emotional devastation of dealing with being an incest survivor. Then there was the constant renegotiation of the relationship with my higher power, much of which I have chronicled in other meditations.

And then a friend asked me, "What about your relationship with yourself?"

It sounded like an invitation to do a little split-personality therapy. I mean, I'm me, right? What's to negotiate?

The answer to that question has involved a lot of work with the Steps, with therapists, and with meditation. It also involves writing, but not the kind I do for a living. If I wanted to get to know the many beings that make up Barry, I was to start a daily exercise of writing three pages every day, longhand, and not for publication.

The first thing I discovered was that I was not used to writing anything more complicated than a check longhand. My handwriting was unreadable, which meant I had to slow down to form the letters clearly, which was the point: slowing down. And then came the process of renegotiating my relationship with myself, beginning with finding out who I am.

Who I am is largely made up out of how I feel, and how I feel is determined by how I see things. How I see things has been revealing. Among many other things, one way I see things startled me. I learned that because of the things I have suffered, I think the universe *owes* me something, and that something appears to be whatever it is that I want. When the things I want don't come to me, I feel personally injured, cheated, gypped.

The terror of my life is rejection, which is especially interesting considering the business I'm in. Let's face it; editors spend most of their working hours rejecting writers. One editor once told me that he rejects pieces of paper, not writers. I told him that if he believes that, I have a choice tract of property on the bottom of Boston Harbor he might be interested in purchasing.

Hence, every rejection is a major slap in the face and an immediate crisis of self-worth. Every story or proposal I send out is a piece of me saying, "How much am I worth?" Each rejection is authority peeing in a snowbank saying, "There. That's what you are worth." It's not a terribly effective way to increase one's serenity.

In other words, how I see things causes me untold mountains of grief. The solution is to drag in that reality check, have a number of little talks with myself, until both of us (or all of us) see things more as they are. It's what the Serenity Prayer calls "courage to change the things I can," which is me and how I see things; and change is what renegotiation is all about.

It's typical of this disease that for all our self-centeredness, the last relationship we look at repairing is the one we have with ourselves. This was best illustrated by my counselor back at rehab. I had dropped in for a return visit after about five years in the program, and in group I was talking about some of the persons I had on my amends list. After I was finished, my counselor asked me, "Is there anyone you forgot to put on your amends list?"

I scoured my brain trying to remember all those to whom I owed amends. In fact, there were some on that list that I wasn't even certain deserved to be there, just to make sure. I didn't know what she was talking about. "I don't think I left anyone off the list," I answered.

"How about yourself?" While I pondered that, she turned to the group and said, "When you make up your amends list in Step Eight, don't forget to place yourself at the top of the list."

152. What's It All Mean?

It hardly ever fails. Get a few drunks or potheads together, pop some tops and light up, and before the puking and paranoia set in, it goes from gaiety, to sloppy sentimentality, and then to self-pity and morose speculation on the meaning of life and other weighty philosophical subjects. In recovery, curiously enough, we often skip the merriment and cut straight to the self-pity and philosophy.

The mental quagmire-dipping usually begins with an incident that can be anything from news about a senseless and brutal murder to a flat tire or a broken fingernail. Crime statistics or political news are good places to start for those having difficulty in triggering a "What's it all mean?" wallow. Most of us, though, have no trouble getting philosophical.

If whatever went wrong today can't do it, whatever went wrong in the past, or might go wrong in the future, will usually do the trick. Eventually we wind up asking ourselves the biggies: What is the purpose of life? What is the meaning of life? What is the point of all the pain in the world? What is the point of all this pain in my life? Why am I here? Is there any point in staying here?

Eventually we get to the question our disease really wants us to consider: Why stay clean, sober, and abstinent? I mean, what's the point? With all of the crap going on in this world, why in the hell should I recover? For what?

When we catch ourselves doing this, we realize that the disease controls the moment, and do what we can to get out of it. We talk it out at a meeting, call a sponsor, do some writing, meditate, or commune with our various higher powers. These things center us, regain our balance, and get us back on track. One thing it doesn't do, however, is answer the questions.

Leaving them unanswered lets the dragon work with them, and one thing I've discovered is that the dragon never has my best interests at heart. One time in early recovery I began the task of answering these questions for myself. I am still working on the answers, and here is my current set:

What is the purpose of life?
Those of us who were listening in high school biology learned that the purpose of life is life. That's what life does: it tries to keep living. That's its purpose. Life has no choice. I do.

What is the meaning of life?
Bad question. It implies that there is only one meaning or significance for everyone. A better question would be, what significance will I give my life? My meaning in life is my choice, and it is something that will change as I grow. What significance my life has and will have in the future is determined by my continuing efforts to become what I was meant to be.

Why am I here?
Okay, first there's this egg, see? Then along comes this pollywog-looking thing called a sperm cell, and it basically jumps the egg; the combination divides and keeps dividing until someone or something stops it. That's why I'm here.

Is there any point in staying here?
One of the ones that can halt all that cell division is me. If I do that, though, I'm never going to become what I was meant to be.

What is the point of all this pain in the world?
Pain is an indicator that something is wrong. More often than not, it is a sign that something needs to be done differently. There is a lot wrong and a lot that needs to be done differently. Pain lingers for want of change.

What is the point of all this pain in my life?
Pain is an indicator that something is wrong. More often than not, it is a sign that something needs to be

done differently. There is a lot wrong and a lot that needs to be done differently. Pain lingers for want of change.

Why stay clean, sober, and abstinent?
It is the only way I can keep those cells dividing so I can become what I was meant to be.

With all of the crap going on in this world, why in the hell should I stay clean and sober?
Actually, I significantly reduced the amount of crap in the world by getting into recovery. I suspect the level will not decrease at all by my going out again. Besides, if I am ever going to be able to lend a hand in decreasing the amount of crap in this world that didn't have anything to do with my using, I need to be alive and able to think. Come to think about it, one of those who help lower the crap level may be what I was meant to be.

153. A Tenth Step Parable

Someone came into a meeting and told this tale:

Once upon a time there was a fellow who decided one day that taking out the garbage was just too much bother. "I'm too busy," he said. "I have more important things to do than take out the garbage. I refuse." So he didn't.

The next day he realized that his not taking out the garbage hadn't stopped the world from spinning.

Things were okay, and he was getting a lot of work done with the time he saved. So he gave the house a shot of air freshener and put off taking out the garbage that day as well.

Five months later as he was burning a rubber tire in his kitchen to cover up the smell, he thought of a few things: "I'm not getting any work done. I'm spending all my time trying to cover up the smell in my house." He took a sniff. "It really does stink in here," he admitted. "Let's see; it's been five months since I took out the garbage. Hmmmm. I guess that's why it stinks. I think I'll take out the garbage."

It took a long time to haul out five months' worth of garbage, but when he was done, he inhaled the fresh air and said, "Gee, taking out the garbage was a good idea. I think I'll do it every day."

And he lived happily ever after; that is, up until the next time he found an excuse for not taking out the garbage.

154. How Many Flashbulbs Does It Take to Screw Up an Addict?

The blue flamers were riding once again, and the members of the Twelve Step meeting were patiently allowing one of them to say his piece, and a brutal piece it was. Time in sobriety means nothing, meetings are not healing places, if you're working the Steps the right way meetings are unnecessary, you have to work the Steps in such-and-such a manner and in such-and-such amount of time, anyone who isn't doing the program such-and-such a way is a fraud, and so on.

It does seem as though there ought to be some sort of net you can throw over some people to cart them off to Happy Valley, but we are taught that there is something to learn from everyone, even if that something is that there is nothing to learn from this jerk.

Finally the person wound down and there was this embarrassed silence while the others in the meeting mentally tried out and discarded choice phrases from earlier days. At last, one old-timer broke the silence by introducing himself and then saying, "When I first came into the program my sponsor told me to stay away from two things: alcohol and flashbulbs. He said to stay away from flashbulbs because they burn very bright, and then they die."

155. The Beatings Will Continue Until Morale Improves

There I was one day, beating myself up because I wasn't happy. It's much like sticking your finger into an electrical socket because you're in so much pain. Have you ever complained about the heat while drinking hot chocolate, or complained about the cold while eating ice cream? When I was in rehab I complained to one of the nurses that I was having difficulty sleeping. She asked me how much coffee

I was drinking. I told her maybe thirty or forty cups a day. "And you're having trouble sleeping? I can't figure that out," she said.

This mode of thinking reaches way beyond the ridiculous when I find myself getting angry because I'm angry or depressed because I'm depressed. In group once, when I was in rehab, I did some very personal sharing. After the session was done, my counselor asked me how I had felt when I was sharing. When I told her that I hadn't felt guilty at all during the sharing, her face brightened up. That ended when I told her that I was feeling real guilty right then for not feeling guilty when I shared.

How come getting clean and sober was like eating a fifty-pound sack of stupid pills? My emotions were all over the place and just as screwy as my thinking. Except for the people I was in recovery with, I didn't have anything to compare it with until I tried to make my personal computer "better."

There was some software on my computer that was giving me problems, and other stuff that took up valuable space. One day I deleted it all, figuring that all of my computer's problems were then over. It is not a coincidence that when I quit using alcohol and other drugs, I figured all my problems were over. In both cases it soon became clear that the problems were just beginning. With the computer, it seems that when the bad stuff went on, it changed a few things and replaced them with something else. When I took the bad stuff off, it no longer was taking up the slack for the stuff it replaced. In addition, it didn't change back the stuff that it had altered. My computer had turned into an anchor with knobs.

Beginning to see the comparison? The addictive use of drugs changed the way my brain did things by getting rid of them and replacing them with other ways of doing things. When I was given cause to be sad, instead of feeling sad or crying, I drank. When I was given cause to be anxious, instead of resolving the problem or accepting the things I cannot change, I ate a few pills. In a million different areas of my life, things in my thinking and behavior were changed until I depended on the regular application of certain drugs to function at all. When the drugs were removed, however, everything didn't automatically snap back to what they were before I used addictively. In other words, I was a zeroed hard drive wondering why I could no longer add two plus two.

Okay, just to finish beating this metaphor to death, I needed new software, and that's what I get from the program: newer and healthier ways of living my life. Now all I need to clear up is my floppy disk condition.

> *Technoweenies sing this song,*
> *Do DOS, do DOS . . .*
>
> *I can see clearly now, the brain is gone . . .*

156. Personal Research

Interesting meeting. The man who was chairing had a familiar opinion: "All of this business about 'If you don't want to slip, stay out of slippery places,' isn't for everyone. Maybe some need it, but I don't. I like to hang out in bars. I like the music and the atmosphere. What's more, that's where all my friends are. The drinking really doesn't bother me. I just sip on my club soda and ignore the drinking and drugging that goes on around me. As a matter of fact, I'm going to do just that tomorrow night. I've been clean for almost eighteen months, so I guess the slippery places thing doesn't apply to me."

A voice from behind me muttered, "It's amazing how, at times, you can almost see a flock of little black bats flying around some people's heads." The comment came from someone who had said essentially the same thing a few months before. Luckily she only totaled her car and had to spend a two-week stretch in the hospital before she made it back into the program. That night she shared that part of her experience, but the previous speaker wasn't listening with both ears. That was the last we saw or heard of him for two years. There were no local newspaper or television reports, no scuttlebutt, nothing. It was as if the earth had swallowed him up.

Twenty-six months later, he came into the meeting late, collected a few hugs, sat down, and then he shared about how he had gone to his favorite bar to listen to the music, and came to several days later in another state and in jail for attempted bank robbery. The court really hadn't taken his crime too seriously, since he didn't have a gun and had been so drunk that a little old lady had to help him out of the bank's lobby to make his getaway. The police picked him up standing on the sidewalk outside the bank; and what was worse, the whole thing was on videotape. Copies of the tape were in hot demand and had already been enjoyed by the officers and prisoners at the jail where he was being held, and more copies made it to the prison where he sat out the remainder of his two years. He did share that it is probably a good idea to stay out of slippery places.

—◆—

It has been said many times: Learning from your own mistakes shows intelligence; learning from the mistakes of others shows wisdom. Still, sometimes there is no substitute for personal research. One fellow in the program was explaining that the reason he couldn't drive to meetings was that his license had been taken away.

"How come?" asked a newcomer.

The guy shrugged and said, "The judge didn't have a sense of humor."

An old-timer nearby said, "I know that judge. He has a sense of humor. He just gets tired hearing the same old joke over and over again."

157. Cool Waters

*If the only prayer you say in your whole life
is "thank you" that would suffice.*
                    —Meister Eckhart

There was a "God of our understanding" meeting I sat in on during which those attending shared about their own brands of spirituality and how they first experienced this "connectedness" to others, to the program, and to a higher power.

The first person who shared related something his sponsor had told him about the subject. "There's only two things you have to know about your higher power: First, it can keep you clean. Second, you're not it."

One woman shared about her first feeling of "connectedness" with others in the program. It was after she had been in a halfway house for a while and realized that all of the women in the halfway house had their menstrual cycles in sync.

Toward the end of the meeting, a woman talked about her frustration with comparing her spirituality with someone else's. "If my sister and I were both in the desert, I wouldn't be able to find a drop of water, but she'd not only get water, she'd get a table to put the damned glass on."

Then someone else at the meeting said something that sounded funny at the time but struck me a moment later as quite profound. He said, "If you ask her, maybe your sister will give you a drink of her water."

We've all heard it put another way: "If you don't believe, believe that I believe." Frankly, asking for the drink of water made more sense to me, and gave me a lot of hope for myself and for all of the brothers and sisters I have in the program who struggle with the higher power issue. Until you settle on a higher power for yourself, you can borrow someone else's. Even more important, my soul can literally feed off of someone else's spirituality. Throughout this book I've related instances in which, through someone else's spiritual strength, insight, or wisdom, my dragon has been chased back into its den, leaving me still on the ride for another day. I've also seen it a thousand times. Someone crawls into a meeting, absolutely crushed, believing in nothing save the final release of a substance-soaked death. Then someone will tell his or her story, or talk about when all was dark and what brought light, and the crawler hears enough to get up and work toward becoming a human being for another twenty-four hours.

Hope. According to my dictionary it means to wish for something with expectation of its fulfillment. The dictionary also lists a couple of obsolete meanings: "to have confidence; trust."

I have seen the kind of hope a child has when writing a Santa Claus letter, and the kind of hope an addict or alcoholic has when trying to score another high. For these, perhaps "to have confidence; trust" are obsolete meanings. I have seen, however, the kind of hope men, women, and children achieve on the threshold of recovery—that first moment in the program when the sufferer realizes there is not only a way out but that there are thousands of eager helping hands as guides. For me, that kind of hope takes the dust off of "to have confidence; trust."

During my years in the program, a number of persons have buttonholed me selling their particular brand of faith. They all said the same thing: "If you have sufficient faith in [God, our beliefs, our leader, this or that particular cult], you wouldn't need to go to all those meetings." This is always said as though doing without those meetings would be, for me, some kind of treat. The catch, however, is always some misunderstanding regarding what amount of faith is "sufficient." I guess I've heard it said over too many corpses, "He just didn't have enough faith."

If I have enough faith? It keeps reminding me of something that was told to me by a great sage many years ago: "If a toad had wings, he wouldn't bump his ass every time he jumped."

Keep coming back for your drink of water. The supply is limitless.

158. The Killing Side

There is a part of me I call "the killing side." It is a two-year-old child throwing a temper tantrum using the body, mind, abilities, and authority of an adult. Turned outward, my killing side revels in revenge fantasies, mischief designed to tear down others, dangerous exhibitions designed to intimidate and impress, and sarcastic little jokes designed to exact payment for some distant wrong. Turned inward, my killing side rejoices in self-loathing, self-punishments for real and imagined wrongs, putting down myself with little jokes designed to make me look as though I don't take myself very seriously.

The killing side is a childish tangle of pain, rage, hurt, desire, and confusion. When it shows itself to me, I am often torn between hammering it into oblivion as though it didn't exist, and letting it loose with the excuse of "getting in touch with my feelings."

An example of the first was the time I was driving my wife to the airport so that she could catch a flight to visit her parents. We were having an enjoyable drive, she leaned over and kissed me, then suddenly there were blue lights flashing at me from my rear view mirror. I looked at the speedometer and I was doing about eighty. Well, I was speeding, and that's a fact. The state trooper was just doing his job, and that's a fact. I pulled over, gave the state trooper a big grin, and that, too, is a fact. I kept an even keel, exercised perfect acceptance, and maintained my serenity, and that is eight yards of prime bullshit. What I did was take that little two year-old inside of me and forbid him to speak, shout, feel, think, or act. I did not let him exist. All that came later.

About a month passed and my wife and I were again driving, this time on our way home. We were on the outskirts of Waterville, Maine, and a cop car was going the other way. My fuzz buster went off, I checked my speed, and I was only doing fifty. I didn't think anymore about it, and we went merrily on our way. In another minute, however, those blue lights were once again flashing at me from my rearview mirror.

I checked the speed again: fifty. I pulled over while my two-year-old tried to decide between being threatened and being ripped off. The cop wanted my license and registration. I told him I was only doing fifty, and he had a comeback that satisfied him: "The speed limit here is twenty-five."

As the cop began walking back to his cruiser to run me through his computer, a volcano of protest began making me shake in anticipation of a major eruption. I made a half-hearted attempt to hold it down, but it was open road in the country and I had not seen any twenty-five MPH sign. Suddenly all of the stuff I had ever been told about not being assertive enough ripped the mountain open and I exploded. I got out of my car, determined to stand up for myself, and began chasing the cop back to his cruiser. He stopped, turned toward me and said, "Please get back in your car."

"I will not!"

"Our insurance doesn't cover you being out of your car."

"That is not my problem!" I yelled.

It's a little hazy from here on. I remember waving my arms about, accusing this guy of running a speed trap. I remember, as well, the cop's partner sitting in the cop car with his hand on a shotgun while I'm screaming at the first cop about not seeing any damned twenty-five MPH sign. The cop is trying to calm me down, and my wife is out of the car, standing there, looking at me, her face nine shades whiter than the Pillsbury Doughboy's. I could see that some future Al-Anon meeting was going to get an earful. At this rather tense moment, my killing side is in full control. I'm looking at this flabby, balding cop, six inches shorter than I am, his hand on the butt of his pistol, and I'm telling myself, *"I can take the little fuck."*

After that, the steam began hissing out of my ears and I started deflating. I had seen, for the very first time, my killing side square in the face. Some deranged two-year-old was running things and had almost gotten me in a punchout with two heavily armed men over a speeding ticket! I slinked back to the car and got in, my face so red from embarrassment that the heat almost melted out the car's windshield.

After communing with his higher power, the cop gave me back my license and registration along with a warning. No ticket. Somehow I think he saw my two-year-old, as well, and took pity. I apologized for my behavior, and at the meeting I attended that night I had some new things to put on my gratitude list: no one shot me or beat my head in, I wasn't in jail, I was alive, and I hadn't hurt or killed anyone else. That was the day I named this unthinking part of me that simply reacts, hurting myself and others, the killing side.

Even today, after much Step work and therapy, the killing side is still with me. I am much more aware of it, however. Now, when it wants to tear loose against myself or others, I don't sit on it and try to make it nothing. Neither do I let it act out. Instead we have a little talk about not being two years old and in the sandbox any longer, that we no longer need to hurt ourselves or others, and that certain behaviors endanger all that we've worked and fought for over the years. Maybe I'll sulk a bit, mutter a lot, have a cry, work out on a heavy bag, write up a storm, feel the feelings and let them go. It's a new life. There is no longer any need to think about killing anyone, including myself.

Through recovery the killing side grows a little smaller, a little less powerful, every day. Part of my continued recovery, though, is to remember that the killing side, although dormant, is always there, ready to come back to life anytime I'm too busy, too bored, or too smart to work my program. I'll stick with the program. It's a lot less bother than wearing a sign around my neck that says, "Danger—Psychotic!"

At a meeting where I shared about the above experience, a program brother put it another way. "People keep telling me to get in touch with my inner child. I don't need to get in touch with my inner child. I *am* my inner child. What I need to get in touch with is my outer adult."

Afterthought

Often it seems as though all the troubles of life waited until we gave up the drink, drug, or other behavior to land on us, but that isn't true. It's only the awareness of those problems that was waiting until our heads cleared. Throughout *Yesterday's Tomorrow* we've looked at problems and ways of dealing with them, not all of which appear in program literature. As you can see, one of the most important tools for dealing with recovery and with life, for me, is laughter. I used to feel guilty about this until something both frightening and depressing happened to me.

It was a new heart problem for me. I had had a heart attack years before, which had left a little something behind: some damaged wiring that resulted in an intermittent rapid heartbeat phenomenon called ventricular tachycardia. After one particularly serious episode, and a scary ambulance ride to the Maine Medical Center in Portland, I found myself in a very frightening place. All of the patients on the floor had serious heart problems, and everyone was wired up such that trained eyes monitored all of our heartbeats twenty-four hours a day. There was hope that my condition could be taken care of with medication. If not, the alternative was a really grim operation.

It looked as though I would be spending Christmas in the hospital. Once again I found myself down at the bottom of a hole and asking my higher power for help. All at once I became very restless. Since I was not confined to my bed, I got up to take a walk around the hallways. It was late in the evening. Visiting hours and meals were all finished. I passed patient rooms, looked in, and saw plenty of persons in worse shape than I was, which was no comfort. I peeked in on the telemetry station where the nurses were watching our heartbeats and asked how I was doing.

"Still some irregularity," came the answer.

With great professionalism and enthusiasm they showed me the records they had of the various dips, spikes, and ratta-tat-tats my heart was performing. They really liked their work, and their eagerness would have been catching except that it was *my* ticker that was the subject of the entertainment.

I continued prowling the floor until I found myself in the patient's lounge. It was deserted, except for a ghoulish display that showed a human heart within a clear plastic torso. The life-sized model was there to show how electrode screens could be mounted right on the walls of my heart and connected to an implanted computer-operated portable defibrillator. The computer monitors the heartbeat, and if it gets irregular, the defib shocks the heart until the pump goes back into normal rhythm. This was the treat waiting for me if my condition couldn't be treated with medication.

It was bizarre having that model in the patient's lounge. The doctors were proud as hell of that thing. The operation, after all, was the house specialty. Patients and visitors, however, either shielded their eyes or turned their heads when they went by the thing. I shook my head and tried to find a magazine to read.

Movie magazines, gardening magazines, women's fashions—soon I found myself looking at the bulletin board wondering when my higher power was going to come up with the help I needed. On the bulletin board were cartoons, clippings, and jokes. There was one clipping, though, that took the guilt out of laughter, turned my moment around, and helped make this book possible. It read:

> *Humor is an affirmation of dignity, a declaration of man's superiority to all that befalls him.*
> —Romain Gary, *Promise at Dawn*

That's when I discovered that humor is not kidding myself out of feelings or a mask I put on to hide the real me from others, although I have used humor to do both. Instead, humor is a way to struggle up off the ground, dust yourself off, and reclaim your life as a valuable human being. So keep coming back. And while you're there, look for the funny bone.

Index

About the Author

Barry Longyear is an award-winning author and sharpened recovery wit. He is the first author to receive the Hugo, Nebula, and John W. Campbell Awards for best new writer within the same year. In his decades of writing and critical acclaim, he has penned many wonderful short stories, science fiction series, mystery novels, and tales of recovery. His works include the *Circus World, Infinity Hold,* and *Enemy Mine* series, among many others. Today, Barry continues his good works in writing and recovery from his home in New Sharon, Maine—the epicenter of his infectious jokes and good cheer.

About Hazelden Publishing

As part of the Hazelden Betty Ford Foundation, Hazelden Publishing offers both cutting-edge educational resources and inspirational books. Our print and digital works help guide individuals in treatment and recovery, and their loved ones. Professionals who work to prevent and treat addiction also turn to Hazelden Publishing for evidence-based curricula, digital content solutions, and videos for use in schools, treatment programs, correctional programs, and electronic health records systems. We also offer training for implementation of our curricula.

Through published and digital works, Hazelden Publishing extends the reach of healing and hope to individuals, families, and communities affected by addiction and related issues.

For more information about Hazelden publications, please call **800-328-9000**
or visit us online at **hazelden.org/bookstore**

Other Titles That May Interest You

Three Simple Rules
Uncomplicating Life in Recovery

BY MICHAEL GRAUBART

Recovery is hard, but it doesn't have to be complicated. The good news is there are just three key things we need to focus on. Trust God. Clean house. Help others. *Three Simple Rules* offers a new take on this valuable slogan and explains how these rules can help anyone find fulfilling recovery. Author Michael Graubart uses wit and wisdom gained in more than twenty years of Twelve Step recovery to explain what worked for him so you can figure out what works for you. In his experience, if you follow the Steps, and focus on the three simple rules, you'll be changed by the process.

Order No. 3655; also available as an ebook

Stepping Stones
More Daily Meditations for Men

In the spiritual successor to the best-selling *Touchstones*, the author continues to explore masculinity and sobriety. This self-help meditation book is designed to help men move forward naturally in their recovery. *Stepping Stones* advances a man's recovery so that it emerges as a comfortable journey that stays in stride with a the rest of his life. It offers insight into the many masculine roles men undertake—father and son, friend and lover—and provides actionable meditations for leading a full life. Life isn't about recovery; recovery is about life.

Order No. 5859; also available as an ebook

Other Titles That May Interest You

Sober Dad
The Manual for Perfectly Imperfect Parenting
BY MICHAEL GRAUBART
2018 Midwest Book Awards Finalist!

Here's your guide to giving up being a "guy" and to becoming a better man, so that you become a better dad. You aren't going to get everything right. You'll soon see that perfection isn't the point, though. Showing up, being present, getting up, and trying again with your eyes wide open and crystal clear—that's what counts. That's what your kids will remember.

Order No. 3017; also available as an ebook

A Man's Way through the Twelve Steps
BY DAN GRIFFIN, MA

In *A Man's Way through the Twelve Steps,* author Dan Griffin uses interviews with men in various stages of recovery, excerpts from relevant Twelve Step literature, and his own experience to offer the first holistic approach to sobriety for men. Readers work through each of the Twelve Steps, learn to reexamine negative masculine scripts that have shaped who they are and how they approach recovery, and strengthen the positive and affirming aspects of manhood.

   A Man's Way through the Twelve Steps offers practical advice and inspiration for men to define their own sense of masculinity and thus heighten their potential for a lifetime of sobriety.

Order No. 4734; also available as an ebook

Hazelden Publishing books are available at fine
bookstores everywhere.

To order from Hazelden Publishing, call **800-328-9000**
or visit **hazelden.org/bookstore.**